ONLY $5.95 / £3.25 EACH!

P9-DDR-132

		Cassettes Quan.	LP Rec Qua.		
Key Languages					
French	202		227	802	
German	203		228	803	
Italian	206		231	806	
Spanish (Castil)	210		235	810	
Spanish (Lat Am)	213		238	813	
Inglés (Engl-Sp)	290		249	890	
Other Languages					
Arabic	218				
Danish	200		225		
Dutch	212		237		
Finnish	201		226		
Japanese	207		232		
Hebrew	205		230	805	
Greek	204		229		
Norwegian	208		233		
Portuguese	214		239		
Russian	209		234	809	
Serbo-Croatian	215				
Swedish	211		236		

English for Visitors		Cassettes	LP BRIT	LP USA	
For French	250		830	246	
For German	260		835	247	
For Italian	280			248	
For Spanish	290			249	
For Danish	300		850		
For Dutch	270				
For Finnish	310		860		
For Japanese	340				
For Norwegian	320		870		
For Swedish	330				

Total Units

This offer may be cancelled without notice when present are depleted.

Name _____

Address _____

City _____

Postal (ZIP) code _____

Total Units _____
☐ from New Jersey at $5.95 ea. _____
☐ from London at £3.25 ea. _____
☐ Plus pronunciation disc No. _____
at $1.00 / 50p ea. _____
Amount _____
N.J. Res. Sales Tax _____
(UK: VAT is included) _____
TOTAL ENCLOSED _____

TRAVEL WITH BERLITZ

Travel Guides

France: *French Riviera, Loire Valley; *Great Britain:* *London;
Greece: *Athens, Corfu, Crete, Rhodes; *Italy:* *Florence,
*Italian Riviera, Rome and the Vatican, Venice; *Mexico:* *Mexico
City; *Netherlands:* *Amsterdam; *Portugal:* Madeira; *Spain:*
Canary Islands, Costa Brava, Costa Dorada and Barcelona,
Costa del Sol and Andalusia, Ibiza and Formentera, Madrid,
Majorca and Minorca; *Yugoslavia:* Dubrovnik and Southern
Dalmatia, Istria and Croatian Coast, Split and Dalmatia;
USSR: Leningrad, Moscow; *Caribbean:* *French West Indies,
*Puerto Rico, *Virgin Islands   * in preparation

Phrase Books

Arabic, Danish, Dutch, European (14 languages), Finnish,
French, German, Greek, Hebrew, Italian, Japanese, Norwegian,
Polish, Portuguese, Russian, Serbo-Croatian, Spanish,
Latin American Spanish, Swahili, Swedish, Turkish

Bilingual Pocket Dictionaries

Danish, Dutch, Finnish, French, German, Italian, Norwegian,
Spanish, Swedish; European Menu Reader

Dual-Language LP Records

Danish, Dutch, Finnish, French, German, Greek, Hebrew,
Italian, Japanese, Norwegian, Portuguese, Russian, Spanish,
Latin American Spanish, Swedish

Dual-Language Cassettes

Arabic, Danish, Dutch, Finnish, French, German, Greek,
Hebrew, Italian, Japanese, Norwegian, Portuguese, Russian,
Serbo-Croatian, Spanish, Latin American Spanish, Swedish

Dual-Language 8-Track Cartridges

French, German, Hebrew, Italian, Russian, Spanish,
Latin American Spanish

Berlitz travel guides, phrase books, dictionaries and audio materials
are also available for travellers speaking Danish, Dutch, Finnish,
French, German, Italian, Japanese, Norwegian, Portuguese, Serbo-
Croatian, Spanish and Swedish. For complete information or a
catalogue, ask your local bookshop or one of the distributors listed
on the back cover. Or write to:

Editions Berlitz S.A., 1, av. des Jordils, 1000 Lausanne 6, Switzerland

BERLITZ®

ITALIAN
FOR TRAVELLERS

By the staff of Editions Berlitz

Library of Congress Catalog Card Number: 74-1977

First revised edition
First printing 1974
Second printing 1975
Third printing 1977
Fourth printing 1977

Printed in Switzerland by Bron SA Lausanne.

Berlitz Trademark Reg. U.S. Patent Office
and other countries – Marca Registrada

Editions Berlitz S.A.
1, avenue des Jordils
1000 Lausanne 6, Switzerland

Preface

In preparing this complete revision of *Italian for Travellers,* we took into consideration a wealth of suggestions and criticisms received by phrase-book users around the world. As a result, this new edition features:

a) a complete phonetic transcription throughout indicating the pronunciation of all words and phrases you'll need to know on your trip

b) special sections showing the replies your listener might give to you. Just hand him the book and let him point to the appropriate phrase. This is especially practical in certain difficult situations (doctor, garage mechanic, etc.).

c) a complete revision of the section on Eating Out to make it even more useful in a restaurant. Italian Swiss items have been included, too.

d) a tipping chart and a more comprehensive reference section in the back of the book.

These are new features. They complement what has become the world's most popular phrase-book series, helping you with:

* all the phrases and supplementary vocabulary you'll need on your trip

* a wide variety of tourist and travel facts, tips and useful information

* audio aids in the form of cassettes, cartridges and LP records (see order form on page 1 or special envelope insert)

* quick reference through colour coding. The major features of the contents are on the back cover. A complete index is found inside.

These are just a few of the practical advantages. In addition, the book will prove a valuable introduction to life in Italy and Switzerland.

There's a comprehensive section on Eating Out, giving translations and explanations for practically anything one would find on an Italian menu; there's a complete Shopping Guide that will enable you to obtain virtually anything you want. Trouble with the car? Turn to the mechanic's manual with its dual-language terms. Feeling ill? Our medical section provides the most rapid communication possible between you and the doctor.

To make the most of *Italian for Travellers,* we suggest that you start with the "Guide to Pronunciation". Then go on to "Some Basic Expressions". This not only gives you a minimum vocabulary; it helps you to pronounce the language. The entire section has been recorded by native speakers. Send for the record (see page 1).

We're particularly grateful to Mrs. Francesca Rahimi and Dr. Giannino Rigolio for their help in the preparation of this book and to Dr. T.J.A. Bennett who devised the phonetic transcription. We also wish to thank the Italian Government Travel Office for its assistance.

We shall be very pleased to receive any comments, criticisms and suggestions that you think may help us in preparing future editions.

Thank you. Have a good trip.

Throughout this book, the symbols illustrated here indicate small sections where phrases have been compiled that your foreign listener might like to say to *you.* If you don't understand him, give him the book and let him point at the phrase in his language. The English translation is just beside it.

A very basic grammar

Articles

There are two genders in Italian – masculine (masc.) and feminine (fem.).

1. *Definite article* (the):

masc. (sing.)	(plur.)
l' before a vowel	gli
lo before z or s + consonant	gli
il before all other consonants	i

l'amico (the friend)	gli amici (the friends)
lo studente (the student)	gli studenti (the students)
il treno (the train)	i treni (the trains)

fem. (sing.)	(plur.)
l' before a vowel	le
la before a consonant	le

l'arancia (the orange)	le arance (the oranges)
la casa (the house)	le case (the houses)

2. *Indefinite article* (a/an):

masc.: un/uno before z or s + consonant*

* When s is followed by a vowel, the masculine articles are il/i (definite) and un (indefinite).

un magazzino	a department store
uno stadio	a stadium

fem.: una/un' before a vowel

una strada	a street
un'amica	a girl friend

3. *Partitive* (some/any): In affirmative sentences and some interrogatives, **some** and **any** are expressed by **di** + definite article, which has the following contracted forms:

masc. (sing.)	(plur.)
dell' before a vowel	degli
dello before z or s + consonant	degli
del before other consonants	dei

fem. (sing.)	(plur.)
dell' before a vowel	**delle**
della before a consonant	**delle**

For other contractions of preposition + definite article, see page 21.

Desidero del vino.	I want some wine.
Vorrei delle sigarette.	I'd like some cigarettes.
Hai degli amici a Roma?	Have you any friends in Rome?

Nouns

Nouns ending in **o** are generally masculine. To form the plural, change **o** to **i**.

il tavolo (the table)	**i tavoli** (the tables)

Nouns ending in **a** are usually feminine. To form the plural, change **a** to **e**.

la casa (the house)	**le case** (the houses)

Nouns ending in **e**—no rule as to gender. Learn each noun individually. Plurals are formed by changing the **e** to **i**.

il piede (the foot)	**i piedi** (the feet)
la notte (the night)	**le notti** (the nights)

Adjectives

They agree with the noun they modify in number and gender. There are two basic types—ending in **o** and ending in **e**.

masc. (sing.)	(plur.)
leggero light (in weight)	**leggeri**
grande big	**grandi**

fem. (sing.)	(plur.)
leggera	**leggere**
grande	**grandi**

They usually follow the noun but certain common adjectives precede the noun.

un caro amico	a dear friend
una strada lunga	a long street

Demonstratives

this	**questo/questa** (contracted to **quest'** before a vowel)
these	**questi/queste** (no contraction)

That/these: follow same system as **dell'/dello/della,** etc.

that	(masc.) **quell', quello, quel/**(fem.) **quell', quella**
these	(masc.) **quegli, quei/**(fem.) **quelle**

Possessive adjectives and pronouns

These agree in number and gender *with the nouns they modify* (or replace). They are almost always used with the definite article.

	Masculine		Feminine	
	singular	plural	singular	plural
my, mine	**il mio**	**i miei**	**la mia**	**le mie**
your, yours	**il tuo**	**i tuoi**	**la tua**	**le tue**
his, her, hers, its	**il suo**	**i suoi**	**la sua**	**le sue**
our, ours	**il nostro**	**i nostri**	**la nostra**	**le nostre**
your, yours	**il vostro**	**i vostri**	**la vostra**	**le vostre**
their, theirs	**il loro**	**i loro**	**la loro**	**le loro**
*your, yours (sing.)	**il suo**	**i suoi**	**la sua**	**le sue**
*your, yours (plur.)	**il loro**	**i loro**	**la loro**	**le loro**

* This is the formal form—used in addressing people you do not know well.

Thus, depending on the context:

il suo cane	can mean	his, her, your dog
la sua auto	can mean	his, her, your car

Personal pronouns

	Subject	Direct Object	Indirect Object	After a Preposition
I	**io**	**mi**	**mi**	**me**
you	**tu**	**ti**	**ti**	**te**
he, it (masc.)	**lui, egli**	**lo**	**gli**	**lui, esso**
she, it (fem.)	**lei, ella, essa**	**la**	**le**	**lei, essa**
we	**noi**	**ci**	**ci**	**noi**
you	**voi**	**vi**	**vi**	**voi**
they (masc.)	**loro, esse**	**li**	**loro**	**loro**
they (fem.)	**loro, esse**	**le**	**loro**	**loro**

Note: There are two forms for "you" in Italian: **tu** (singular) is used when talking to relatives, close friends and children (and between young people); the plural of **tu** is **voi**. **Lei** is used in all other cases (with the 3rd person singular of the verb).

Verbs

Learn these two auxiliary verbs:

Infinitive:	
essere (to be)	**avere** (to have)
Present tense:	
io* sono (I am)	**io ho** (I have)
tu sei (you are)	**tu hai** (you have)
lui, lei è (he, she, it is)	**lui, lei ha** (he, she, it has)
lei è (you are)	**lei ha** (you have)
noi siamo (we are)	**noi abbiamo** (we have)
voi siete (you are)	**voi avete** (you have)
essi sono (they are)	**essi hanno** (they have)

* The subject pronouns are seldom used except for emphasis.

Regular verbs follow one of three patterns:

Infinitive:	ends in **-are**	ends in **-ere**	ends in **-ire**
	comprare (to buy)	**vendere** (to sell)	**partire** (to leave)
Present tense:			
io	compro	vendo	parto
tu	compri	vendi	parti
lui, lei	compra	vende	parte
noi	compriamo	vendiamo	partiamo
voi	comprate	vendete	partite
essi	comprano	vendono	partono

Here are four useful irregular verbs:

Infinitive:	**andare** (to go)	**potere** (to be able)	**vedere** (to see)	**fare** (to make)
io	vado	posso	vedo	faccio
tu	vai	puoi	vedi	fai
lui, lei	va	può	vede	fa
noi	andiamo	possiamo	vediamo	facciamo
voi	andate	potete	vedete	fate
essi	vanno	possono	vedono	fanno

Negatives

Negatives are formed by putting **non** before the verb.

Non vado a Roma.   I am not going to Rome.

Questions

In Italian, questions are often formed by simply changing the inflexion of your voice. Remember that the personal pronoun is rarely used, either in affirmative sentences or in questions.

Parlo italiano.   I speak Italian.
Parla italiano?   Do you speak Italian?

Prepositions

There is a list of prepositions on page 16. Note the following contractions.

Definite Article	**a** at, to	**da** by, from	**di** of	**in** in	**su** on	**con** with
+ il	al	dal	del	nel	sul	col
+ l'	all'	dall'	dell'	nell'	sull'	con l'
+ lo	allo	dallo	dello	nello	sullo	con lo
+ la	alla	dalla	della	nella	sulla	con la
+ i	ai	dai	dei	nei	sui	coi/con i
+ gli	agli	dagli	degli	negli	sugli	con gli
+ le	alle	dalle	delle	nelle	sulle	con le

Guide to pronunciation

This and the following chapter are intended to make you familiar with the phonetic transcription we devised and to help you get used to the sounds of Italian.

As a minimum vocabulary for your trip, we've selected a number of basic words and phrases under the title "Some Basic Expressions" (pages 10–15). That selection serves another purpose. Recorded by native speakers of Italian, it forms the script for our pronunciation record (see page 1).

An outline of the spelling and sounds of Italian

You'll find the pronunciation of the Italian letters and sounds explained below, as well as the symbols we're using for them in the transcriptions. Note that Italian has some diacritical letters—letters with accent marks—which we don't know in English.

The imitated pronunciation should be read as if it were English except for any special rules set out below. Of course, the sounds of any two languages are never exactly the same; but if you follow carefully the indications supplied here, you'll have no difficulty in reading our transcriptions in such a way as to make yourself understood.

Letters written in bold should be stressed (pronounced louder).

Consonants

Letter	Approximate pronunciation	Symbol	Example	
b, d, f, k, l, m, n, p, q, t, v	are pronounced as in English			
c	1) before e and i, like ch in chip	ch	cerco	chayrkoa
	2) elsewhere, like c in cat	k	conto	koantoa

ch	like **c** in **c**at	k	**che**	kay
g	1) before **e** and **i**, like **j** in **j**et	j	**leggero**	laydjairoa
	2) elsewhere, like **g** in **g**o	g	**grande**	**grahn**day
gh	like **g** in **g**o	g	**ghiaccio**	geeahtchoa
gl	like **lli** in mi**lli**on	ly	**gli**	lyee
gn	like **ni** in o**ni**on	ñ	**bagno**	**bah**ñoa
h	always silent		**ha**	ah
r	trilled like a Scottish **r**	r	**caro**	**kar**roa
s	1) generally like **s** in **s**it	s/ss	**questo** **casa**	kooaystoa **kar**ssah
	2) sometimes like **z** in **z**oo	z	**viso**	**vee**zoa
sc	1) before **e**, **i**, like **sh** in **sh**ut	sh	**uscita**	oo**shee**tah
	2) elsewhere, like **sk** in **sk**in	sk	**scarpa**	**skahr**pah
z or **zz**	1) generally like **ts** in hi**ts**	ts	**grazie**	**grart**seeay
	2) sometimes like **ds** in roa**ds**	dz	**romanzo**	roa**mahn**dzoa

Vowels

a	1) short, like **ar** in c**ar**, but shorter	ah	**gatto**	**gaht**toa
	2) long, like **ar** in c**ar**	ar	**casa**	**kar**ssah
e	1) can always be pronounced like **ay** in g**ay**	ay	**sera**	**say**rah
	2) in correct speech, it is sometimes pronounced like **e** in g**e**t or, when long, more like **air** in h**air**	eh ai	**bello** **bene**	**behl**loa **bai**nay
i	like **ee** in m**ee**t	ee	**vini**	**vee**nee
o	1) can always be pronounced like **oa** in g**oa**t	oa	**sole**	**soa**lay
	2) in correct speech, it is sometimes pronounced like **o** in g**o**t, or when long, more like **aw** in l**aw**	o aw	**notte** **rosa**	**not**tay **raw**zah
u	like **oo** in f**oo**t	oo	**fumo**	**foo**moa

Two or more vowels

In groups of vowels **a, e,** and **o** are strong vowels, and **i** and **u** are weak vowels. When two strong vowels are next to each other, they are pronounced as two separate syllabes, e.g., *beato* = bay**ah**toa. When a strong and weak vowel are next to each other, the weak one is pronounced more quickly and with less stress (less loudly) than the strong one, e.g., *piede* = pee**ay**day; such sounds are diphthongs and constitute only one syllable. If the weak vowel is stressed, then it is pronounced as a separate syllable, e.g., *due* = **doo**ay. Two weak vowels together are pronounced as a diphthong, and it is generally the second one that is more strongly stressed, e.g., *guida* = goo**ee**dah.

Stressing of words

Generally, the vowel of the next to the last syllable is stressed. When a final vowel is stressed, it has an accent written over it *(più)*. Normally an accent is used only when the stress falls on a final vowel, and not when it falls on syllables before the next to the last one.

Some basic expressions

Yes.	**Sì.**	see
No.	**No.**	no
Please.	**Per piacere.**	pair peeah**chay**ray
Thank you.	**Grazie.**	**grart**seeay
Thank you very much.	**Molte grazie.** **Tante grazie.**	**moal**tay **grart**seeay **tahn**tay **grart**seeay
That's all right.	**Va bene.**	vah **bai**nay
You're welcome.	**Prego.**	**pray**goa

Greetings

Good morning.	**Buongiorno.**	bwon**joar**noa
Good afternoon.	**Buongiorno.**	bwon**joar**noa
Good evening.	**Buona sera.**	**bwo**nah **say**rah
Good night.	**Buona notte.**	**bwo**nah **not**tay
Good-bye.	**Arrivederci.**	ahrreevayday**dair**chee
So long!	**Ciao!**	**char**oa
See you later.	**A più tardi.**	ah peeoo **tahr**dee
This is Mr. ...	**Le presento il signor...**	lay pray**zayn**toa eel see**ñoar**
This is Mrs. ...	**Le presento la signora...**	lay pray**zayn**toa lah see**ñoar**ah
This is Miss...	**Le presento la signorina...**	lay pray**zayn**toa lah seeñoar**ee**nah

How do you do?	**Molto lieto.**	**moalt**oa **leeayt**oa
I'm very pleased to meet you.	**Sono molto lieto di fare la sua cono-scenza.**	**soan**oa **moalt**oa **leeayt**oa dee **farray** lah **sooah koan**oa**ashehnt**sah
How are you?	**Come sta?**	**koam**ay stah
Very well, thanks.	**Molto bene, grazie.**	**moalt**oa **bain**ay **grartseeay**
And you?	**E lei?**	ay laiee
How's it going?	**Come va?**	**koam**ay vah
Excuse me. (I didn't hear.)	**Mi scusi.**	mee **skooz**ee
Excuse me. (May I get past?)	**Permesso?**	pairmaisssoa
That's all right.	**Non importa.**	noan eemportah
I beg your pardon?	**Come dice?**	**koam**ay **deech**ay

Questions

Where?	**Dove?**	**doa**vay
Where is...?	**Dov'è...?**	**doa**vai
Where are...?	**Dove sono...?**	**doa**vay **soan**oa
When?	**Quando?**	**kwahnd**oa
What?	**Che cosa/Che?**	kay **kawss**ah/kay
How?	**Come?**	**koam**ay
How much?	**Quanto?**	**kwahnt**oa
How many?	**Quanti?**	**kwahnt**ee
Who?	**Chi?**	kee
Why?	**Perchè?**	pehr**kay**
Which?	**Quale?**	**kwar**lay

What do you call this in Italian?	**Come si chiama questo in italiano?**	koamay see keearmah kooaystoa een eetahleearnoa
What do you call that in Italian?	**Come si chiama quello in Italiano?**	koamay see keearmah kooaylloa een eetahleearnoa
What do you call these in Italian?	**Come si chiamano questi in italiano?**	koamay see keearmahnoa kooaystee een eetahleearnoa
What does this mean?	**Che cosa significa questo?**	kay kawssah seeñeefeekah kooaystoa
What does that mean?	**Che cosa significa quello?**	kay kawssah seeñeefeekah kooaylloa

Do you speak...?

Do you speak...?	**Parla...?**	pahrlah
Do you speak English?	**Parla inglese?**	pahrlah eengglayssay
Is there anyone here who speaks...?	**C'è qualcuno qui che parla...?**	chai kwahlkoonoa kooee kay pahrlah
I don't speak much Italian.	**Non parlo bene l'italiano.**	noan pahrloa bainay leetahleeanoa
Could you speak more slowly?	**Può parlare più lentamente, per favore?**	pwo pahrlarray peeoo layntahmayntay pair fahvoaray
Could you repeat that?	**Vuol ripetere, per favore?**	vwol reepaitayray pair fahvoaray
Please write it down.	**Per favore, me lo scriva.**	pair fahvoaray may loa skreevah
Can you translate this for me?	**Può tradurmi questo?**	pwo trahdoormee kooaystoa
Please point to the phrase in the book.	**Per favore, mi indichi la frase nel libro.**	pair fahvoaray mee eendeekee lah frarzay nehl leebroa
Just a minute. I'll see if I can find it in this book.	**Un attimo, per favore. Guardo se posso trovarla in questo libro.**	oon ahtteemoa pair fahvoaray. gwahrdoa say posssoa troavarrlah een kooaystoa leebroa

I understand.	**Capisco.**	kahpeeskoa
I don't understand.	**Non capisco.**	noan kahpeeskoa
Do you understand?	**Capisce?**	kahpeeshay

Can...?

Can I have...?	**Posso avere...?**	posssoa ahvayray
Can we have...?	**Possiamo avere...?**	possseearmoa ahvayray
Can you show me...?	**Può mostrarmi...?**	pwo moastrarrmee
I can't.	**Non posso.**	noan posssoa
Can you tell me...?	**Può dirmi...?**	pwo deermee
Can you help me?	**Può aiutarmi?**	pwo ighootarrmee
Can I help you?	**Posso aiutarla?**	posssoa ighootarrlah
Can you direct me to...?	**Può indicarmi la direzione per...?**	pwo eendeekahrmee lah deeraytseeoanay pair

Wanting

I'd like...	**Vorrei...**	vorraiee
We'd like...	**Vorremmo...**	vorrehmmoa
What do you want?	**Che cosa desidera?**	kay kawssah dayzeedayrah
Give me...	**Mi dia...**	mee deeah
Give it to me.	**Me lo dia.**	may loa deeah
Bring me...	**Mi porti...**	mee portee
Bring it to me.	**Me lo porti.**	may loa portee
Show me...	**Mi mostri...**	mee moastree
Show it to me.	**Me lo mostri.**	may loa moastree

I'm looking for...	**Cerco...**	**chayr**koa
I'm hungry.	**Ho fame.**	oa **far**may
I'm thirsty.	**Ho sete.**	oa **say**tay
I'm tired.	**Sono stanco.**	**soa**noa **stahng**koa
I'm tired.*	**Sono stanca.**	**soa**noa **stahng**kah
I'm lost.	**Mi sono perduto.**	mee **soa**noa pehr**doo**toa
It's important.	**È importante.**	ai eempor**tahn**tay
It's urgent.	**È urgente.**	ai oor**jehn**tay
Hurry up!	**Presto!**	**prehs**toa

It is/There is...

It is/It's...	**È...**	ai
Is it...?	**È...?**	ai
It isn't...	**Non è...**	noan ai
There it is.	**Eccolo.**	**ehk**koaloa
There you are!	**Eccoti!**	**ehk**koatee
Here they are.	**Eccoli/Eccole.**	**ehk**koalee/**ehk**koalay
There it is.	**Eccolo.**	**ehk**koaloa
There they are.	**Eccoli.**	**ehk**koalee
There is/There are...	**Vi è/Vi sono...**	vee ai/vee **soa**noa
Is there/Are there...?	**C'é/Ci sono...?**	chai/chee **soa**noa
There isn't/There aren't...	**Non c'è/Non ci sono...**	noan chai/noan chee **soa**noa
There isn't any.	**Non ce n'è.**	noan chay nai
There aren't any.	**Non ce ne sono.**	noan chay nay **soa**noa

* Said by a woman.

It's...

big/small	**grande/piccolo**	grahnday/peekkoaloa
quick/slow	**rapido/lento**	rarpeedoa/lehntoa
early/late	**presto/tardi**	prehstoa/tahrdee
cheap/expensive	**buon mercato/caro**	bwawn mayrkahtoa/karroa
near/far	**vicino/lontano**	veecheenoa/lontarnoa
hot/cold	**caldo/freddo**	kahldoa/frayddoa
full/empty	**pieno/vuoto**	peeaynoa/**vwaw**toa
easy/difficult	**facile/difficile**	farcheelay/deffeecheelay
heavy/light	**pesante/leggero**	payssahntay/laydjairoa
open/shut	**aperto/chiuso**	ahpehrtoa/keeoossoa
right/wrong	**giusto/sbagliato**	joostoa/zbahlyartoa
old/new	**vecchio/nuovo**	vehkkeeoa/nwawvoa
old/young	**anziano/giovane**	ahntseeahnoa/joavahnay
next/last	**prossimo/scorso**	prossseemoa/skorsoa
beautiful/ugly	**bello/brutto**	bailloa/broottoa
free (vacant)/occupied	**libero/occupato**	leebayroa/okkoopartoa
good/bad	**buono/cattivo**	bwawnoa/kahtteevoa
better/worse	**migliore/peggiore**	meelyoaray/paydjoaray
here/there	**qui/là**	kooee/lah
now/then	**adesso/dopo**	ardaisssoa/dawpoa

Quantities

a little/a lot	**un po'/molto**	oon po/moaltoa
much/many	**molto/molti**	moaltoa/moaltee
more than/less than	**più di/meno di**	peeoo dee/mainoa dee
enough/too	**abbastanza/troppo**	ahbbahstahntsa/troppoa
some (any)	**qualche**	kwahlkay

A few prepositions and some more useful words

at	**a**	ah
on	**su**	soo
in	**in**	een
to	**a**	ah
from	**da**	dah
inside	**dentro**	dayntroa
outside	**fuori**	fwawree
up/upstairs	**su, in alto/di sopra**	soo een ahltoa/dee soaprah
down/downstairs	**giù/di sotto**	joo/dee soattoa
for	**per**	payr
after	**dopo**	dawpoa
before (time)	**prima**	preemah
before (place)	**davanti**	dahvahntee
with	**con**	kon
without	**senza**	sayntsah
through	**per/attraverso**	pair/ahttrahvehrsoa
towards	**verso**	vehrsoa
until	**fino a**	feenoa ah
during	**durante**	doorahntay
and	**e**	ay
or	**o**	oa
not	**non**	noan
nothing	**nulla/niente**	noollah/neeayntay
none	**nessuno**	naysssoonoa
very	**molto**	moaltoa
too (also)	**anche**	ahngkay
soon	**presto**	prehstoa
perhaps	**forse**	forsay

Arrival

You've arrived. Whether you've come by ship or plane, you'll have to go through passport and customs formalities. (For car/border control, see page 146.)

There's certain to be somebody around who speaks English. That's why we're making this a brief section. What you really want is to be off to your hotel in the shortest possible time. And here are the steps to get these formalities out of the way quickly.

Passport control

In these days of the jumbo jet, you may well be waved through passport control with a smile. Otherwise:

Here's my passport.	**Ecco il passaporto.**	ehkkoa eel pahsssahportoa
I'll be staying...	**Resterò...**	raystayroa
a few days	**qualche giorno**	kwahlkay joarnoa
a week	**una settimana**	oonah saytteemarnah
two weeks	**due settimane**	dooay saytteemarnay
a month	**un mese**	oon maizay
I don't know yet.	**Non so ancora.**	noan soa ahngkoarah
I'm here on holiday.	**Sono qui in vacanza.**	soanoa kooee een vahkahntsah
I'm here on business.	**Sono qui per affari.**	soanoa kooee pair ahffarree
I'm just passing through.	**Sono di passaggio.**	soanoa dee pahsssadjeeoa

If things become difficult:

I'm sorry, I don't understand.	**Mi dispiace, non capisco.**	mee deespeeahchay noan kahpeeskoa
Is there anyone here who speaks English?	**C'è qualcuno qui che parla inglese?**	chai kwahlkoonoa kooee kay pahrlah eengglayssay

Customs

The chart below shows what you can bring in duty-free (visitors from overseas are allowed greater concessions as regards duty-free cigarettes and tobacco).*

	Cigarettes		Cigars		Tobacco (grams)	Spirits (liquor) (lit.)		Wine (lit.)
Italy	300	or	75	or	400	1½	and	3
Switzerland	200	or	50	or	250	1	and	2

At almost all major airports in Europe, an honour system for clearing customs has been adopted. Baggage is often not even opened, although spot checks are a possibility. After collecting your baggage, you have a choice: follow the green arrow if you've nothing to declare. Or leave via a doorway marked with a red arrow if you've items to declare (in excess of those allowed).

MERCI DA DICHIARARE
GOODS TO DECLARE

NULLA DA DICHIARARE
NOTHING TO DECLARE

I've nothing to declare.	**Non ho nulla da dichiarare.**	noan oa **noo**llah dah deekeeah**rar**ray
I've a...	**Ho una...**	oa **oo**nah
carton of cigarettes	**stecca di sigarette**	**stayk**kah dee seegah**rayt**tay
bottle of whisky	**bottiglia di whisky**	bot**teel**yah dee whisky
Must I pay on this?	**Devo pagare per questo?**	**day**voa pah**gar**ray pair **koo**aystoa
It's for my personal use.	**È per mio uso personale.**	ai pair **mee**oa **oo**zoa pairsoa**nar**lay

* All allowances subject to change without notice and measurements are approximate. Although customs officers hardly ever quibble about the difference between a litre bottle and a quart bottle, they are, of course, entitled to stick to the letter of the law if they choose.

Il passaporto, per favore.	Your passport, please.
Ha qualche cosa da dichiarare?	Do you have anything to declare?
Per favore, apra questa borsa.	Please open this bag.
Deve pagare il dazio per questo.	You'll have to pay duty on this.
Ha altri bagagli?	Do you have any more luggage?

Baggage – Porters

The porter may take your bags to customs for you. He'll then wait till they've been cleared. Note the number on his badge.

Porter!	**Facchino!**	fahkkeenoa
Please take these bags.	**Per favore, prenda queste borse.**	pair fahvoaray prehndah kooaystay borsay
That's mine.	**Quella è la mia.**	kooayllah ai lah meeah
That's my...	**Quella è...**	kooayllah ai
bag	**la mia borsa**	lah meeah borsah
luggage	**il mio bagaglio**	eel meeoa bahgarlyoa
suitcase	**la mia valigia**	lah meeah vahleejah
That...one.	**Quella...**	kooayllah
big/small	**grande/piccola**	grahnday/peekkoalah
blue/brown	**blu/marrone**	bloo/mahrroanay
black/plaid	**nera/scozzese**	nayrah/skoattsayssay
There's one piece missing.	**Manca un collo.**	mahnkah oon kolloa
Take these bags to the...	**Porti queste borse...**	portee kooaystay borsay
bus	**all'autobus**	ahllowtoabooss
luggage lockers	**alla custodia auto- matica dei bagagli**	ahllah koostawdeeah owtoamarteekah daiee bahgarlyee
taxi	**al taxi**	ahl tahsssee
How much is that?	**Quanto le devo?**	kwahntoa lay dayvoa

Note: The normal rate is 150 lire per bag. Have some small change ready.

ARRIVAL

Changing money

You'll find a bank at most airports. If it's closed, don't worry. You'll be able to change money at your hotel.

Full details about money and currency exchange are given on pages 134–136.

Where's the nearest currency exchange?	**Dove si trova l'ufficio cambio più vicino?**	doavay see trawvah loof-feecheeoa kahmbeeoa peeoo veecheenoa
Can you change these traveller's cheques (checks)?	**Può cambiare questi traveller's cheques?**	pwo kahmbeearray kooaystee traveller's cheques
I want to change some…	**Vorrei cambiare…**	vorraiee kahmbeearray
dollars	**dei dollari**	daiee dollahree
pounds	**delle sterline**	dayllay stayrleenay
Can you change this into lire?	**Può cambiare questo in lire?**	pwo kahmbeearray kooaystoa een leeray
What's the exchange rate?	**Qual'è il corso del cambio?**	kwahlai eel korsoa dayl kahmbeeoa

Directions

How do I get to…?	**Come posso andare a…?**	koamay posssoa ahndarray ah
Where's the bus to the centre of town?	**Dov'è l'autobus che va in centro?**	doavai lowtoabooss kay vah een tchayntroa
Where can I get a taxi?	**Dove posso prendere un taxi?**	doavay posssoa prayndayray oon tahsssee
Where can I hire (rent) a car?	**Dove posso noleggiare un'automobile?**	doavay posssoa noalaydjarray oonowtoa-mawbeelay

Hotel reservations

Many terminals have a hotel reservation service or tourist information office. You're sure to find someone there who speaks English. There's sometimes a special telephone that connects you to a hotel service or to individual hotels.

FOR NUMBERS, see page 175

ARRIVAL

Car rental

There are car rental firms at most airports and terminals. It's highly likely that someone there will speak English. But if nobody does, try one of the following:

I'd like a...	**Vorrei noleggiare una...**	vorraiee noalaydjeearray oonah
car	**macchina**	mahkkeenah
small car	**macchina piccola**	mahkkeenah peekkoalah
large car	**macchina grande**	mahkkeenah grahnday
sports car	**macchina sportiva**	mahkkeenah sporteevah
I'd like it for...	**La vorrei per...**	lah vorraiee pair
a day	**un giorno**	oon joarnoa
four days	**quattro giorni**	kwahttroa joarnee
a week	**una settimana**	oonah saytteemarnah
What's the charge per...?	**Qual'è la tariffa...?**	kwahlai lah tahreeffah
day	**giornaliera**	joarnahleeayrah
week	**per una settimana**	pair oona saytteemarnah
Does that include mileage?	**Compreso il chilometraggio?**	koamprayssoa eel keelawmaytrahdjeeoa
What's the charge per kilometre?	**Qual'è la tariffa al chilometro?**	kwahlai lah tarreeffah ahl keelawmaytroa
Is petrol (gasoline) included?	**È incluso il prezzo della benzina?**	ai eengkloozoa eel prehtsoa dayllah bayndzeenah
I want full insurance.	**Voglio l'assicurazione completa.**	volyoa lahssseekooraht-seeoanay koamplaytah
What's the deposit?	**Quanto è la cauzione?**	kwahntoa ai lah kowtseeoanay
I've a credit card.	**Ho una carta di credito.**	oa oonah karrtah dee kraydeetoa
Here's my driving licence.	**Ecco la mia patente.**	ehkkoa lah meeah partehntay

Note: In Italy a translation of your own licence or an international licence is required.

FOR SIGHTSEEING, see page 75

Taxi

All taxis have meters. It's usually best to ask the approximate fare beforehand. For some trips (e.g., airport to town) there may be a fixed rate. This will be posted at the airport. From 10 p.m. to 7 a.m. there's a night supplement which isn't indicated on the meter.

Where can I get a taxi?	**Dove posso trovare un taxi?**	doavay posssoa trawvahray oon tahsssee
Please get me a taxi.	**Per favore, mi trovi un taxi.**	pair fahvoaray mee trawvee oon tahsssee
What's the fare to…?	**Qual'è il prezzo della corsa fino a…?**	kwahlai eel prehttsoa dayllah korsah feenoa ah
How far is it to…?	**Quanto dista…?**	kwahntoa deestah
Take me to…	**Mi conduca a…**	mee koandookah ah
this address the town centre the…Hotel	**questo indirizzo in centro città all'albergo…**	kooaystoa eendeereettsoa een chayntroa cheettah ahllahlbayrgoa
Turn…at the next corner.	**Al prossimo angolo giri…**	ahl prossseemoa ahnggoloa jeeree
left/right	**a sinistra/a destra**	ah seeneestrah/ah dehstrah
Go straight ahead.	**Vada sempre diritto.**	vahdah sehmpray deereettoa
Please stop here.	**Per favore si fermi qui.**	pair fahvoaray see fayrmee kooee
I'm in a hurry.	**Ho fretta.**	oa frayttah
Could you drive more slowly?	**Può andare più lentamente?**	pwo ahndarray peeoo lehntahmayntay
Could you help me to carry my bags?	**Può aiutarmi a portare le mie borse?**	pwo ighootarrmee ah portahray lay meeay borsay

ARRIVAL

Hotel—Other accomodation

Early reservation (and confirmation) is essential in most major tourist centres during the high season. Most towns and arrival points have a tourist information office (*azienda di soggiorno e turismo*—ahdzee**ehn**dah dee sod**joar**noa ay too**ree**smoa), and that's the place to go if you're stuck without a room.

It's wise to remember that various surcharges may be added to your hotel bill; the Italian tourist organization, E.N.I.T., publishes an annual directory of all hotels in Italy with details of minimum and maximum prices and facilities.

albergo (ahl**bayr**goa)	The usual word for "hotel" in Italian is *albergo*. Hotels in Italy are classified as *di lusso* (dee **looss**soa– international luxury class) or first, second, third or fourth class.
appartamento ammobiliato (ahppahrtah**maynt**oa ahmmoabeelee**ah**toa)	Furnished flat (apartment). Contact a specialized travel agent if this is the type of arrangement you're looking for.
locanda (lo**kahn**dah)	A country inn.
motel (mo**tehl**)	Increasing in number, improving in service, the Automobile Association of Italy has a list of recommended motels.
pensione (paynsee**oa**nay)	Corresponds to a boarding house; it usually offers *pensione completa*(...koam**play**tah—full board) or *mezza pensione* (**mehd**dzah...—half board). Meals are likely to be from a set menu. *Pensione* are classified first, second or third class.

Note: Especially near railway stations, one often finds *alberghi diurni* (ahl**bayr**gee dee**oor**nee—"daytime hotels"). These have no sleeping accomodation, but provide bathrooms, rest rooms, hairdressers, and other similar services. Most close at midnight.

FOR YOUTH HOSTELS/CAMPING, see page 89

In this section, we're mainly concerned with the smaller and medium-priced hotels and boarding houses. You'll have no language difficulties in the luxury and first-class hotels where most of the staff speak English.

In the next few pages we consider your requirements—step by step—from arrival to departure. You needn't read all of it; just turn to the situation that applies.

Checking in – Reception

My name is…	**Mi chiamo…**	mee keearmoa
I've a reservation.	**Ho fatto una prenotazione.**	oa **fah**ttoa **oo**nah praynoatahtseeoanay
We've reserved two rooms, a single and a double.	**Abbiamo prenotato due camere, una singola e una matrimoniale.**	ahbbeearmoa praynoatah-toa **doo**ay **kar**mayray **oo**nah **seeng**goalah ay **oo**nah mahtreemoneeahlay
I wrote to you last month.	**Vi ho scritto il mese scorso.**	vee oa **skreet**toa eel **mai**zay **skor**soa
Here's the confirmation.	**Ecco la conferma.**	**ehk**koa lah konfehrmah
I'd like a…room…	**Vorrei una camera…**	vorraiee **oo**nah **kar**mayrah
single	**singola**	**seeng**goalah
double	**matrimoniale**	mahtreemoneeahlay
with twin beds	**con due letti**	kon **doo**ay **leh**ttee
with a bath	**con bagno**	kon **bar**ñoa
with a shower	**con doccia**	kon **dot**chah
with a balcony	**con terrazzo**	kon tayrrattsoa
with a view	**con vista**	kon **vee**stah
I'd like a suite.	**Vorrei un appartamento.**	vorraiee oon ahppahrtah-mayntoa
We'd like a room…	**Vorremmo una camera…**	vorrehmmoa **oo**nah **kar**mayrah
in the front	**sul davanti**	sool dah**vahn**tee
at the back	**sul retro**	sool **rai**troa
facing the sea	**sul mare**	sool **mar**ray
facing the courtyard	**sul cortile**	sool korteelay

HOTEL

HOTEL

It must be quiet.	**Deve essere tranquilla.**	dayvay ehsssayray trahngkooeellah
Is there...?	**C'è...?**	chai
air conditioning	**l'aria condizionata**	larreeah kondeetseeonartah
heating	**il riscaldamento**	eel reeskahldahmayntoa
a radio/television in the room	**la radio/il televisore nella stanza**	lah rardeeoa/eel taylayvee-zoaray nayllah stahntsah
laundry service	**il servizio di lavanderia**	eel sayrveetseeoa dee lah-vahndayreeah
room service	**il servizio nella stanza**	eel sayrveetseeoa nayllah stahntsah
hot water	**l'acqua calda**	lahkkwah kahldah
running water	**l'acqua corrente**	lahkkwah korraintay
a private toilet	**il gabinetto privato**	eel gahbeenayttoa preevahtoa

How much?

What's the price...?	**Qual'è il prezzo...?**	kwahlai eel prehttsoa
per week	**per una settimana**	pair oonah saytteemarnah
per night	**per una notte**	pair oonah nottay
for bed and breakfast	**per la camera e la colazione**	pair lah karmayrah ay lah koalahtseeoanay
excluding meals	**pasti esclusi**	parstee ayskloozee
for full board	**per la pensione completa**	pair lah paynseeoanay koamplaytah
for half board	**per mezza pensione**	pair mehdzah paynseeoanay

Does that include...?	**Il prezzo comprende...?**	eel prehttsoa koampraynday
breakfast	**la colazione**	lah koalahtseeoanay
meals	**i pasti**	ee parstee
service	**il servizio**	eel sayrveetseeoa
value-added tax*	**l'I.V.A.**	leevah
Is there any reduction for children?	**C'è una riduzione per i bambini?**	chai oonah reedootsee-oanay pair ee bahmbeenee
Do you charge for the baby?	**Fate pagare per il bambino?**	fahtay pahgarray pair eel bahmbeenoa
That's too expensive.	**È troppo caro.**	ai troppoa karroa
Haven't you anything cheaper?	**Non ha nulla di meno caro?**	noan ah noollah dee mainoa karroa

* Americans note: a type of sales tax.

FOR NUMBERS, see page 175

How long?

We'll be staying...	**Resteremo...**	raystayraymoa
overnight only	**una notte**	oonah nottay
a few days	**qualche giorno**	kwahlkay joarnoa
a week (at least)	**una settimana (come minimo)**	oonah saytteemarnay (koamay meeneemoa)
I don't know yet.	**Non ho ancora deciso.**	noan oa ahngkoarah daycheessoa

Decision

May I see the room?	**Posso vedere la camera?**	posssoa vaydayray lah karmayrah
No, I don't like it.	**No, non mi piace.**	noa noan mee peeahchay
It's too...	**È troppo...**	ai troppoa
cold / hot	**fredda / calda**	frayddah / kahldah
dark / small	**buia / piccola**	booeeah / peekkoalah
noisy	**rumorosa**	roomoaroazah
I asked for a room with a bath.	**Ho chiesto una camera con bagno.**	oa keeehstoa oonah karmayrah kon barñoa
Do you have anything...?	**Ha qualcosa...?**	ah kwahlkawssah
better / bigger	**migliore / più grande**	meelyoaray / peeoo grahnday
cheaper	**meno caro**	mainoa karroa
quieter	**più tranquillo**	peeoo trahngkooeelloa
higher up	**più in alto**	peeoo een ahltoa
lower down	**più in basso**	peeoo een bahsssoa
Do you have a room with a better view?	**Ha una camera con una vista più bella?**	ah oonah karmayrah kon oonah veestah peeoo baillah
That's fine. I'll take it.	**Va bene, la prendo.**	vah bainay lah prehndoa

HOTEL

Bills

These are usually paid weekly. Most hotels offer a reduction for children under 12.

FOR DAYS OF THE WEEK, see page 181

HOTEL

Tipping

A service charge (15–20%) is normally included in the bill, but you can ask:

Is service included?	**È compreso il servizio?**	ai koam**prayss**oa eel sayr**veet**seeoa

It is customary to leave some tips on top of this—see our suggestions on the inside back-cover.

Registration

Upon arrival in a hotel or boarding house you'll be asked to fill in a registration form (*una scheda*— **oo**nah **skay**dah). It asks your name, home address, passport number and further destination. It's almost certain to carry an English translation. If it doesn't, ask the desk-clerk (*portiere*– poartee**ay**ray):

What does this mean?	**Cosa significa questo?**	**kaw**ssah see**ñee**feekah **koo**aystoa

The desk-clerk will ask you for your passport. He may want to keep it for a while. Don't worry. You'll get it back.

Mi può mostrare il passaporto?	May I see your passport?
Vuol compilare la scheda, per cortesia?	Would you mind filling in this registration form?
Firmi qui, per favore.	Sign here, please.
Quanto tempo si trattiene?	How long will you be staying?

What's my room number?	**Qual'è il numero della mia stanza?**	kwah**lai** eel **noo**mayroa **dayl**lah **mee**ah **stahn**tsah
Will you have our bags sent up?	**Vuole portare i nostri bagagli in camera?**	**vwaw**lay por**tar**ray ee **nos**tree bar**gah**lyee een **kar**mayrah

Service, please

bellboy	**inserviente ai piani**	eensayrveeayntay ahee peeahnee
maid	**cameriera (nelle camere)**	kahmayreeayrah
manager	**direttore**	deerayttoaray
room service	**valletto**	vahllayttoa
switchboard operator	**centralinista**	chayntrarleeneestah
waiter	**cameriere**	kahmayreeayray
waitress	**cameriera**	kahmayreeayrah

Call the members of the staff *signore, signorina* or *signora.*
Address the waiter as *cameriere* when calling for service.

General requirements

Please ask the maid to come up.	**Per favore, dica alla cameriera di salire.**	pair fahvoaray deekah ahllah kahmayreeayrah dee sahleeray
Who is it?	**Chi è?**	kee ai
Just a minute.	**Un attimo.**	oon artteemoa
Come in!	**Avanti.**	ahvahntee
Is there a bath on this floor?	**C'è la stanza da bagno a questo piano?**	chai lah stahntsah dah barñoa ah kooaystoa peearnoa
How does this shower work?	**Come funziona questa doccia?**	kawmay foontseeoanah kooaystah dotchah
Where's the plug for the shaver?	**Dov'è la spina per il rasoio?**	doavai lah speenah pair eel rarzoaeeoa
Can we have breakfast in our room?	**Possiamo avere la colazione in camera?**	possseearmoa ahvayray lah koalahtseeoanay een karmayrah
I'd like to leave these in your safe.	**Vorrei depositare questi nella vostra cassaforte.**	vorraiee daypozeetarray kooaystee nayllah vostrah kahsssahfortay
Can you find me a baby-sitter?	**Può trovarmi una baby-sitter?**	pwo trawvahrmee oonah "baby-sitter"

HOTEL SERVICE

SUONARE PER IL SERVIZIO
RING FOR SERVICE

May I have a/an/some…?	Posso avere…?	posssoa ahvayray
ashtray	un portacenere	oon portahchaynayray
bath towel	un asciugamano da bagno	oon ahshoogarmarnoa dah barñoa
extra blanket	una coperta in più	oonah kopehrtah een peeoo
hangers	degli attaccapanni	daylyee ahttahkkahparnnee
ice cubes	dei cubetti di ghiaccio	daiee koobehttee dee geeahtchoa
extra pillow	un guanciale in più	oon gwahncharlay een peeoo
reading-lamp	una lampada	oonah lahmpahdah
soap	del sapone	dayl sahpoanay
Where's the…?	Dov'è…?	doavai
barber's	il barbiere	eel bahrbeeehray
bathroom	la stanza da bagno	lah stahntsah dah barñoa
dining-room	la sala da pranzo	lah sarlah dah prahndzoa
hairdresser's	la parrucchiera	lah pahrrookkeeayrah
restaurant	il ristorante	eel reestorahntay
television room	la sala della televisione	lah sarlah dayllah taylay-veezeeoanay
toilet	il gabinetto	eel garbeenaytttoa

Breakfast

The Italian breakfast consists of coffee, *brioches* (bree**osh**), *focaccia* (foa**kaht**cheeah—crisp buns and flaky pastry) and *marmellata* (mahrmayl**lar**tah—jam). Some hotels can also provide an English or American breakfast.

I'll have a/an/some…	Desidero…	dayzeedayroa
bacon and eggs	uova e pancetta	ooawvah ay pahnchehttah
cereal	dei fiocchi d'avena	daiee feeokkee darvaynah
hot/cold	caldi/freddi	kahldee/frayddee
eggs	delle uova	dayllay ooawvah
boiled egg	uovo alla coque	ooawvoa ahllak kok
soft/medium/hard	molli/mezza cottura/sode	mollee/mehddzah kottoorah/soday
fried eggs	uova fritte	ooawvah freettay
scrambled eggs	uova strapazzate	ooawvah straahpahttsartay

fruit juice	un succo di frutta	oon sookkoa dee froottah
grapefruit / orange	pompelmo/arancia	pompaylmoa/ahrahn-chah
ham and eggs	prosciutto e uova	proashoottoa ay ooawvah
jam	della marmellata	dayllah mahrmayllartah
marmalade	della marmellata d'arance	dayllah mahrmayllartah dahrahnchay
omelet	una frittata	oonah freettartah
pancakes	delle frittelle	dayllay freettehllay
toast	un toast	oon "toast"
yoghurt	uno yogurt	oonoa eeawgoort
May I have some…?	Posso avere un po' di…?	posssoa ahvayray oon po dee
hot milk / cold milk	latte caldo/latte freddo	lahttay kahldoa/lahttay frayddoa
cream / sugar	panna/zucchero	pahnnah/tsookkayroa
bread / rolls	pane/panini	parnay/parneenee
butter	burro	boorroa
salt / pepper	sale/pepe	sarlay/paipay
coffee / tea	caffè/tè	kahffai/tai
chocolate	cioccolato	choakkaolartoa
lemon / honey	limone/miele	leemoanay/meeaylay
hot water	acqua calda	ahkkwah kahldah
Could you bring me a…?	Può portarmi…?	pwo portarmee
plate	un piatto	oon peeahttoa
glass / cup	un bicchiere/una tazza	oon beekkeeayray/oonah tahttsah
knife	un coltello	oon koltehlloa
fork	una forchetta	oonah forkehttah
spoon	un cucchiaio	oon kookkeeighoa

Difficulties

The…doesn't work.	…non funziona.	noan foontseeoanah
air-conditioner	il condizionatore d'aria	eel koandeetseoanahtoaray darreeah
fan	il ventilatore	eel vaynteelahtoaray
heating	il riscaldamento	eel reeskahldahmayntoa
light	la luce	lah loochay
radio	la radio	lah rardeeoa
tap	il rubinetto	eel roobeenayttoa
toilet	il gabinetto	eel gahbeenayttoa
ventilator	la ventilazione	lah vaynteelahtseeoanay

HOTEL SERVICE

FOR EATING OUT, see pages 38–64

The wash-basin is clogged.	**Il lavabo è otturato.**	eel lahvarboa ai ottoorartoa
The window is jammed.	**La finestra è incastrata.**	lah feenehstrah ai eengkahstrartah
The blind is stuck.	**L'imposta è bloccata.**	leempoastah ai blokkartah
These aren't my shoes.	**Queste non sono le mie scarpe.**	kooaystay noan soanoa lay meeay skahrpay
This isn't my laundry.	**Questa non è la mia biancheria.**	kooaystah noan ai lah meeah beeahngkayreeah
There's no hot water.	**Non c'è acqua calda.**	noan chai ahkkwah kahldah
I've lost my watch.	**Ho perso l'orologio.**	oa pairsoa loaroaloioa
I've left my key in my room.	**Ho lasciato la chiave nella mia stanza.**	oa lahsheeartoa lah keearvay nayllah meeah stahntsah
The...is broken / burned out.	**...è rotto (rotta).**	...ai rottoa (rottah)
bulb	**la lampadina**	lah lahmpahdeenah
lamp	**la lampada**	lah lahmpahdah
plug	**la spina**	lah speenah
shutter	**l'imposta**	leempoastah
switch	**l'interruttore**	leentayrroottoaray
venetian blind	**la persiana alla veneziana**	lah pairseearnah ahllah vaynaytseearnah
window shade	**la tendina**	lah taydeenah
Can you get it repaired?	**Può ripararlo?**	pwo reepahrahrloa

Telephone – Mail – Callers

Can you get me Rome 123–45–67?	**Può passarmi Roma 123–45–67?**	pwo pahsssahrmee roamah 123–45–67
Did anyone telephone me?	**Mi ha telefonato qualcuno?**	mee ah taylayfoanartoa kwahlkoonoa
Do you have stamps?	**Ha dei francobolli?**	ah daiee frahngkoaboallee
Would you please mail this for me?	**Può spedirmi questo, per favore?**	pwo spaydeermee kooaystoa pair fahvoaray
Are there any messages for me?	**Vi sono messaggi per me?**	vee soanoa maysssahdjee pair may

FOR POST OFFICE and TELEPHONE, see pages 137–141

Checking out

May I please have my bill?	**Posso avere il conto, per favore?**	**poss**soa ahvayray eel **koan**toa pair fahvoaray
I'm leaving early tomorrow. Please have my bill ready.	**Partirò domani mattina presto. Mi prepari il conto, per favore.**	pahrteeroa doamarnee mahtteenah **prehs**toa. mee prayparree eel **koan**toa pair fahvoaray
We'll be checking out around noon.	**Partiremo verso mezzogiorno.**	pahrteeraymoa **vehr**soa mehdzoajoarnoa
I must leave at once.	**Devo partire immediatamente.**	**day**voa pahrteeray eemmaydeeahtah**mayn**tay
Is everything included?	**È tutto incluso?**	ai **toot**toa eenkloozoa
You've made a mistake in this bill, I think.	**Ha fatto un errore nel conto, credo.**	ah **faht**toa oon ehrroray nayl **koan**toa craydoa
Can you get us a taxi?	**Può chiamarci un taxi?**	pwo keeah**mahr**chee oon tahsssee
When's the next... to Naples?	**A che ora parte il prossimo...per Napoli?**	ah kay oarah **pahr**tay eel **pross**seemoa...pair narpoalee
bus/train/plane	**autobus/treno/aereo**	owtoaboos/**tray**noa/ahairayoa
Would you send someone to bring down our baggage?	**Può mandare qualcuno a portare giù i nostri bagagli?**	pwo mahn**dar**ray kwahl**koo**noa ah portarray joo ee nostree bahgahlyee
We're in a great hurry.	**Abbiamo molta fretta.**	ahbbeearmoa **moal**tah **frayt**tah
Here's the forwarding address.	**Ecco il mio prossimo indirizzo.**	**ehk**koa eel meeoa **pross**seemoa eendee**reet**tsoa
You have my home address.	**Avete il mio indirizzo abituale.**	ah**vay**tay eel meeoa eendee**reet**tsoa ahbeetooarlay
It's been a very enjoyable stay.	**È stato un soggiorno molto piacevole.**	ai **star**toa oon soadjoarnoa **moal**toa peeah**chay**voalay
I hope we'll come again sometime.	**Spero che ritorneremo ancora.**	**spay**roa kay reetornayray**ray**moa ahngkoarah

HOTEL SERVICE

FOR TAXI, see page 27

Eating out

There are various types of places to eat and drink in Italy. Here are some of them:

Autogrill
(owtoagreel)

Large restaurant on a motorway (turnpike); usually table and cafeteria service available.

Bar

Bar; can be found on virtually every street corner; coffee and drinks served. In most of them you first have to get a ticket from the cashier's. Then you go to the counter and order what you want. Only a few bars have tables and chairs. If you want to be served at a table, the charge for your drinks and food will be somewhat higher. A sign in the window reading *tavola calda* means that simple hot dishes are served.

Caffè
(kahffai)

Coffee shop; generally food isn't served there except for breakfast. If it offers *panini o toasts* you'll be able to get a snack. Coffee shops always serve alcoholic beverages.

Gelateria
(jaylahtayreeah)

Ice-cream parlour; Italian ice-cream is very tasty, rich and creamy, often reminiscent of old-fashioned, homemade ice-cream.

Locanda
(lokahndah)

Simple restaurants serving local dishes.

Osteria
(oastayreeah)

Inn; wine and sometimes simple food is served.

Pizzeria
(peettsayreeah)

Pizza parlour; often other dishes are served, too.

Ristorante
(reestoarahntay)

Restaurant; this is the more sophisticated type of eating place. You'll encounter restaurants classified by stars, forks and knives and endorsed by everyone including travel agencies, automobile associations and gastronomic guilds. Bear in mind that any form of classification is relative. Some restaurants are judged according to their fancy décor while others—linen and chandeliers aside—are rated merely by the quality of their cooking.

Rosticceria
(roasteetchayreeah)

Originally, it was a shop specializing in grilled meats, chicken and fish. But today *rosticcerias* often have tables where you eat grilled food on the premises.

Taverna
(tahvehrnah)

A more modest type of *trattoria*.

Tea-room

Serves ice-cream and pastries.

Trattoria
(trahttoareeah)

A medium-priced restaurant serving meals and drink. The food is simple but can be surprisingly good if you happen to hit upon the right place.

Meal times

In this section, we're primarily concerned with lunch and dinner. We assume that you've already had breakfast at your hotel or boarding house. See page 34 for a breakfast menu.

Lunch (*il pranzo*—eel **prahn**dzoa) is served from 12.30 to 3 p.m.

Dinner (*la cena*—lah **chay**nah) is usually served later in Italy than at home, seldom beginning before 8 p.m.

The Italians like to linger over a meal so service may seem on the leisurely side. Restaurants close one day per week, often on Monday.

EATING OUT

Eating habits

Most restaurants display a menu in the window. Many offer a tourist menu (*menù turistico*), and you'll often find a *piatto del giorno* (pee**aht**toa dayl **joar**noa—dish of the day) too which usually offers you a good meal at a fair price. Words like *del ristorante* or *del cuoco* next to a dish listed on the menu are clues that the dish is a speciality of the restaurant. If the menu mentions *vino incluso,* it means that wine is included in the price of the meal.

The service charge *(servizio)* of usually 12 to 15 per cent, and even the tip *(mancia),* are almost always shown as being included. If the tip isn't included it's entirely up to you. For a snack you may leave some small change, and if you have enjoyed a good meal you may care to leave about 5 per cent on the table for the waiter. Note that you will occasionally also find one or both of the following items added to your bill: *coperto* (cover charge), *supplemento* (surcharge).

Cosa desidera?	What would you like?
Le consiglio questo.	I recommend this.
Cosa desidera da bere?	What would you like to drink?
Non abbiamo...	We haven't got...
Vuole...?	Do you want...?

Hungry?

I'm hungry/I'm thirsty.	Ho fame/Ho sete.	oa farmay/oa saytay
Can you recommend a good restaurant?	Può consigliarmi un buon ristorante?	pwo koanseelyahrmee oon bwon reestoarahntay
Are there any inexpensive restaurants around here?	Vi sono dei ristoranti economici qui vicino?	vee soanoa daiee reestoarahntee aykoanawmeechee kooee veecheenoa

If you want to be sure of getting a table in a well-known restaurant, it may be better to telephone in advance.

I'd like to reserve a table for 4 people.	**Vorrei riservare un tavolo per 4.**	vorraiee reessayrvarray oon tarvoaloa pair 4
We'll come at 8.	**Verremo alle 8.**	vayrraymoa ahllay 8

Asking and ordering

Good evening. I'd like a table for 3.	**Buona sera. Vorrei un tavolo per 3.**	bwonah sayrah. vorraiee oon tarvoaloa pair 3
Could we have a table...?	**Potremmo avere un tavolo...?**	poatraymmoa ahvayray oon tarvoaloa
in the corner	**d'angolo**	dahnggoaloa
by the window	**vicino alla finestra**	veecheenoa ahllah feenaystrah
outside	**all'aperto**	ahllahpehrtoa
on the terrace	**sulla terrazza**	soollah tayrrahttsah
Where are the toilets?	**Dove sono i gabinetti?**	doavay soanoa ee gahbeenayttee
May I please have the menu?	**Per favore, mi può dare il menù?**	pair fahvoaray mee pwo darray eel maynoo
What's this?	**Cos'è questo?**	kawssai kooaystoa
Do you have...?	**Avete...?**	avaytay
a set menu	**un menù a prezzo fisso**	oon maynoo ah prehttsoa feesssoa
local dishes	**piatti locali**	peeahttee lokarlee
I'd like...	**Vorrei...**	vorraiee
Is service included?	**È compreso il servizio?**	ai koamprayssoa eel sayrveetseeoa
Could we have a/an..., please?	**Potremmo avere..., per favore?**	poatraymmoa ahvayray... pair fahvoaray
ashtray	**un portacenere**	oon portahchaynaray
another chair	**un'altra sedia**	oonahltrah saideeah
glass	**un bicchiere**	oon beekkeeairay
knife	**un coltello**	oon koaltehlloa
napkin	**un tovagliolo**	oon toavahlyawloa
plate	**un piatto**	oon peeahttoa
serviette	**un tovagliolo**	oon toavahlyawloa
spoon	**un cucchiaio**	oon kookkeeighoa
toothpick	**uno stuzzicadenti**	oonoa stoottseekahdehntee

I'd like a/an/some...	Vorrei...	vorraiee
aperitif	un aperitivo	oon ahpayreeteevoa
appetizer	un antipasto	oon ahnteeparstoa
beer	una birra	oonah beerrah
bread	del pane	dayl parnay
butter	del burro	dayl boorroa
cabbage	dei cavoli	daiee karvoalee
chips (Br.)	delle patatine fritte	dayllay pahtahteenay freettay
cheese	del formaggio	dayl foarmahdjoa
coffee	un caffè	oon kahffai
dessert	un dessert	oon dayssssehrt
eggs	delle uova	dayllay wawvah
fish	del pesce	dayl payshay
french fries	delle patatine fritte	dayllay pahtahteenay freettay
fruit	della frutta	dayllah froottah
game	della cacciagione	dayllah kahtchahjoanay
ice-cream	un gelato	oon jaylartoa
iced water	dell'acqua ghiacciata	dayllahkkwah geeahtchartah
lemon	un limone	oon leemoanay
lettuce	della lattuga	dayllah lahttoogah
meat	della carne	dayllah kahrnay
milk	del latte	dayl lahttay
mineral water	dell'acqua minerale	dayllahkkwah meenayrarlay
mustard	della mostarda	dayllah moastahrdah
(olive) oil	dell'olio (d'oliva)	dayllawlyoa (doleevah)
pepper	del pepe	dayl paypay
potatoes	delle patate	dayllay pahtartay
poultry	del pollo	dayl poalloa
rice	del riso	dayl reessoa
rolls	dei panini	daiee pahneenee
salad	dell'insalata	daylleensahlartah
salt	del sale	dayl sarlay
seafood	dei frutti di mare	daiee froottee dee marray
seasoning	del condimento	dayl koandeemayntoa
soup	una minestra	oonah meenehstrah
starter	un antipasto	oon ahnteeparstoa
sugar	dello zucchero	daylloa tsookkayroa
tea	un tè	oon tay
vegetables	delle verdure	dayllay vehrdooray
vinegar	dell'aceto	dayllahchaytoa
water	dell'acqua	dayllahkkwah
wine	del vino	dayl veenoa

What's on the menu?

Our menu is presented according to courses. Under the headings below you'll find alphabetical lists of dishes that might be offered on an Italian menu with their English equivalent. You can also show the book to the waiter. If you want some fruit, for instance, show him the appropriate list and let *him* point to what's available. Use pages 41 and 42 for ordering in general.

Here, then, is our guide to good eating and drinking. Turn to the section you want.

Obviously, you're not going to go through every course on the menu. If you've had enough, say:

Nothing more, thanks. **Nient'altro, grazie.** neeehntahltroa grartseeay

Italian cooking remains essentially regional. Each of the nation's 18 regions has its own specialities. The vicinity of Bologna—Emilia Romagna—is renowned for its culinary art. There are, of course, many well-known dishes that are common to all Italy. But here again the terminology may vary from place to place. (There are at least half a dozen names for octopus or squid!) So in the lists that follow, be prepared for regional variations.

EATING OUT

Appetizers

I'd like an appetizer.	**Vorrei un antipasto.**	vorraiee oon ahnteeparstoa
acciughe	ahtchoogay	anchovies
affettati misti	ahffayttartee meestee	cold cuts of pork
antipasto misto	ahnteeparstoa meestoa	assorted appetizer
carciofi	kahrchofee	artichoke
caviale	kahveearlay	caviar
culatello	koolahtaylloa	smoked pork
frutti di mare	froottee dee marray	mixed seafood
gamberetti	gahmbayrayttee	shrimps
mortadella	moartahdehllah	Bologna sausage
olive	oleevay	olives
farcite	fahrcheetay	stuffed
nere	nehray	black
verdi	vayrdee	green
ostriche	ostreekay	oysters
prosciutto	proashoottoa	ham
affumicato	ahffoomeekartoa	smoked ham
cotto	kottoa	cooked ham
crudo	kroodoa	cured ham
di cinghiale	dee cheenggeearlay	cured wild boar
salame	sahlarmay	salami
tartufi/trifoli	tahrtoofee / treefoalee	(white) truffles

Appetizer specialities

bagna cauda
(bañah kahoodah)

Raw. vegetables accompagnied by a hot sauce made from anchovies, garlic, oil, butter and sometimes truffles (Piedmont and Italian-speaking Switzerland)

insalata di mare
(eenssahlartah dee marray)

prawns and squid with lemon, pickles and olives

mozzarella in carrozza
(moattsahrayllah een karrottsah)

a fried open-faced sandwich of mozzarella cheese dipped in egg

soppressata
(soappraysssartah)

sausage made from pig's head (southern Italy)

torta pasqualina
(toartah pahskooahleenah)

artichoke pie with eggs, mushrooms and Parmesan cheese

zucchini ripieni
(isookkeenee reepeeaynee)

stuffed baby marrows (zucchini)

Pizza

Along with *pasta*, this open pie with its plenitude of different fillings is surely Italy's best known culinary export.

A *pizza* (plural *pizze*) may be covered with tomatoes, ham, anchovies, capers, cheese etc. The cheese is *mozzarella*. It's baked at a very high temperature—and must be eaten hot out of the oven. Since the latter is generally open you can watch your *pizza* sizzling succulently while you wait. It won't burn because it's been lightly brushed with olive oil before being placed on the long, metal spatula over the charcoal embers.

Naples is the great place for *pizza*, and here are the best known variations on the theme:

capricciosa (kahpreet**cho**assah)	The cook's speciality
margherita (mahrgay**ree**tah)	Named after Italy's first queen, the pizza ingredients, tomato, cheese and basil, reflect the national colours
napoletana (nahpoalay**tar**nah)	The classic pizza with anchovies, ham, capers, tomatoes, cheese and oregano
siciliana (seecheel**yar**nah)	With black olives, capers and cheese

Soups

In Italian, soup goes by various names, as the following list shows. Some of these soups may be main-course fare.

brodetto	braw**dayt**toa	broth with beaten eggs and lemon juice
brodo	**braw**doa	bouillon
di manzo	dee **mahnd**zoa	meat
di pollo	dee **poal**loa	chicken
buridda	boo**reed**dah	spicy fish stew
busecca	boo**zayk**kah	tripe with vegetables and seasoning
cacciucco	kah**chook**koa	spicy seafood stew (chowder)
minestra asciutta	meeneh**strah ahshoot**tah	macaroni or rice

minestrina in brodo con fegatini di pollo	meeneh**stree**nah een **braw**doa kon faygah-**tee**nee dee po**alloa**	noodles and chicken livers
minestrone	meeneh**stroa**nay	a thick vegetable soup sprinkled with parmesan cheese
passato di verdura	pahsss**ar**toa dee vehr**doo**rah	vegetable soup
zuppa	**tsoo**ppah	soup
alla cacciatora	**ah**llah kahtchah**toa**rah	meat with mush-rooms
alla marinara	**ah**llah mahreen**arr**ah	spicy fish stew (chowder)
alla veneta	**ah**llah **vay**naytah	vegetables with white wine and noodles
di datteri di mare	dee **daht**tayree dee **marr**ay	seafood
di fagioli	dee **fah**joalee	haricot beans
di frutti di mare	dee **froot**tee dee **marr**ay	seafood
di pesce	dee **pay**shay	spicy fish stew (chowder)
di vongole	dee **vong**goalay	clams and white wine

Pasta

Pasta, the generic name for a wide range of noodles and noodle-related dishes, constitutes the traditional Italian first course. Pasta comes in a bewildering variety of sizes and shapes—ribbons, strings, tubes, shells or stars—known under as many different appellations. It can be served on its own, in broth, stuffed with meat, cheese or vegetables or baked in a pie, and is often accompagnied by a highly flavoured sauce such as those found on page 53.

You'll certainly recognize *cannelloni, maccheroni, ravioli* and *spaghetti,* but some of the names of the dishes on a menu are hard to spot as being pasta. Here are a few favourite pasta dishes you may want to try: *agnoletti, canederli* (a speciality of Trentino-Alto Adige), *cappelletti, fettuccine, lasagne al forno, panzarotti, pappardelle con la lepre* (speciality of Tuscany), *tagliatelle* and *tortellini.*

Rice

Particularly in northern Italy, a rice dish is offered as a first course and often replaces the pasta in a meal. Cooked until very tender together with vegetables, meat, herbs, fish and/or seafood, rice may also be served with a sauce.

risi e bisi	reessee ay beessee	rice with peas and bacon (Venice)
riso in bianco	reessoa een beeahngkoa	boiled rice
risotto	reessottoa	rice casserole
con funghi	kon foonggee	with mushrooms
alla milanese	ahllah meelahnehssay	marrow and white wine

Eggs and omelets

I'd like an omelet.	**Vorrei una frittata.**	vorraiee oonah freettartah
frittata	freettartah	omelet
alla trentina	ahllah traynteenah	artichokes, parsley, basil and marjoram
di carciofi	dee kahrchofee	artichokes
di cipolle	dee cheepoallay	onion
di spinaci	dee speenarchee	spinach
di zucchini	dee tsookkeenee	dried baby marrow (zucchini)
frittatine piemontesi	freettahteenay peeaymoan-tehssee	a thin omelet with Fontina cheese and cream

Fish and seafood

Don't miss the opportunity to sample some of the wide variety of fresh fish and seafood in coastal areas. Some inland regions offer special preparations of fish from their rivers, lakes and streams. Fish is most commonly baked or poached until just done, then dressed with a delicate sauce.

I'd like some fish.	**Vorrei del pesce.**	vorraiee dayl payshay
What kind of seafood do you have?	**Che genere di frutti di mare avete?**	kay jehnayray dee froottee dee marray ahvaytay
acciughe	ahtchoogay	anchovies
aguglie	ahgoolyay	garfish
anguilla	ahnggooeellah	eel

FOR OTHER EGG DISHES, see page 34

EATING OUT

aragosta	ahrahgoastah	crawfish
aringa	ahreenggah	herring
arselle	ahrsehllay	scallops
baccalà	bahkkahlah	dried salt cod
bianchetti	beeahngkayttee	whitebait
branzino	brahndzeenoa	(sea) bass
calamaretti	kahlahmahrayttee	baby squid
calamari	kahlahmarree	squid
carpa	kahrpah	carp
cozze	koatsay	mussels
dentice	dehnteechay	type of sea bream
eperlano	aypayrlarnoa	smelt
gamberetti	gahmbayrayttee	prawns/crayfish
gamberi	gahmbayree	lobster
granchi	grahngkee	crab
gronghi	groanggee	conger eel
lamprede	lahmprayday	lampreys
luccio	lootchoa	pike
lumache di mare	loomarkay dee marray	sea snails
merlano	mayrlarnoa	whiting
merluzzo	mayrloottsoa	cod
muggine	moodjeenay	grey mullet
nasello	nahssehlloa	coal-fish
orata	oarartah	type of sea bream
ostriche	ostreekay	oysters
passerino	pahsssayreenoa	plaice
pesce persico	payshay pehrseekoa	perch
pesce spada	payshay spardah	swordfish
pianuzza	peeahnoottsah	plaice
polpo	poalpoa	octopus
razza	rahttsah	ray
ricci	reetchee	sea urchins
rombo	roamboa	turbot
salmone	sahlmoanay	salmon
San Pietro	sahn peeehtroa	John Dory
sardine	sahrdeenay	sardines
scampi	skahmpee	prawns
scorfano	skoarfahnoa	sea-scorpion/sculpin
sgombro	zgoambroa	mackerel
seppia	sayppeeah	cuttlefish
sogliola	sawlyoalah	sole
spigola	speegoalah	sea bass
storione	stoareeoanay	sturgeon
tonno	toannoa	tunny (tuna)
triglie	treelyay	red mullet
trota	trawtah	trout
vongole	vonggoalay	clams

To make sure you get your fish served the way you want it, refer to the following list:

baked	**al forno**	ahl **for**noa
boiled	**lesso**	**lay**sssoa
(deep) fried	**(ben) fritto**	(bain) **freet**toa
grilled	**alla griglia**	**ahl**lah **greel**yah
marinated	**marinato**	mahreen**ar**toa
poached	**affogato**	ahf**foag**artoa
smoked	**affumicato**	ahffoomee**kar**toa
steamed	**cotto a vapore**	**kott**oa ah vah**poa**ray
stewed	**in umido**	een **oom**eedoa

Seafood specialities

anguilla alla veneziana
(ahnggoo**eel**lah **ahl**lah vaynayt**see**arnah)

eel cooked in sauce made from tunny (tuna) and lemon (Venice)

baccalà alla vicentina
(bahk**kah**lah **ahl**lah veech**ayn**teenah)

cod cooked in milk with onion, garlic, parsley, anchovies and cinnamon (Venice)

fritto misto
(**freet**toa **mees**toa)

a fry of various small fish and shellfish

pesci in carpione
(**pay**shee een kahrpee**oa**nay)

boiled fish, cooked in vinegar, served cold with lemon

pesci al cartoccio
(**pay**shee ahl kahr**tot**choa)

baked in a parchment envelope with onions, parsley and herbs

polpi in purgatorio
(**poal**pee een poorgah**tor**eeoa)

octopus cooked in oil, with tomatoes, parsley, garlic and peppers (Abruzzi)

seppie con carciofi
(**sayp**peeay kon kahr**cho**fee)

cuttlefish with artichoke (Latium)

sgombri in umido
(**zgoam**bree een **oom**eedoa)

stewed mackerel in white wine with green peas

stoccafisso
(stoakkah**fees**soa)

dried cod cooked with tomatoes, olives and artichoke

sogliole alla mugnaia
(**saw**lyolay **ahl**lah moo**ña**reeah)

sole sautéed in butter, garnished with parsley and lemon

triglie alla livornese
(**tree**lyay **ahl**lah leevoar**nay**ssay)

baked red mullet

Meat

I'd like some...	Vorrei...	vorraiee
beef	**del manzo**	dayl **mahn**dzoa
lamb	**dell'agnello**	dayllah**ñeh**lloa
pork	**del maiale**	dayl mi**ghar**lay
veal	**del vitello**	dayl vee**tehl**loa

animelle di vitello	ahnee**mehl**lay dee vee**tehl**loa	sweetbreads
arrosto di manzo	ahr**roas**toa dee **mahn**dzoa	roast beef
bistecca	bee**stayk**kah	steak
di filetto	dee fee**leht**toa	rib steak
braciola	brah**choa**lah	chop
costola	**kos**toalah	rib
costoletta	koastoa**layt**tah	cutlet
cervello	chayr**vehl**loa	brains
fegato	**fay**gahtoa	liver
filetto	fee**layt**toa	fillet
lingua	**leeng**gwah	tongue
lombata/lombo	loam**bar**tah / **loam**boa	loin
midollo	mee**doal**loa	marrow
montone	moan**toa**nay	mutton
pancetta affumicata	pahn**cheht**tah ahffoomee-**kar**tah	bacon
polpette	poal**payt**tay	meatballs
porchetta	poar**kayt**tah	sucking pig
prosciutto	proa**shoot**toa	ham
rognoni	roa**ñoa**nee	kidneys
salumi	sah**loo**mee	assorted pork products
salsicce	sahl**seet**chay	sausages
scaloppina	skahloap**pee**nah	scallop
spalla	**spahl**lah	shoulder
trippe	**treep**pay	tripe
zampa	**tsahm**pah	pig's trotter (feet)

Italian meat dishes

Meat is virtually always dressed with some sort of creamy sauce or gravy—sometimes prepared at your table.

abbacchio (ahb**bahk**keeoa)	roast lamb, often served in a casserole with anchovies (Latium)
bistecca alla fiorentina (bee**stayk**kah ah**llah** feeoararyn**tee**nah)	a grilled steak flavoured with lemon juice and parsley (Tuscany)

cima alla genovese
(**cheemah ahl**lah jaynoavayssay)
rolled veal stuffed with eggs, sausage and mushrooms (Liguria)

corda
(**kor**dah)
lamb tripe roasted or in tomato sauce with green peas (Sardinia)

costata al prosciutto
(koa**star**tah ahl proa**shoot**toa)
a chop filled with ham, cheese and truffles; breaded and fried until golden brown (Emilia-Romagna)

costoletta alla milanese
(koastoa**layt**tah **ahl**lah meelah-**nay**ssay)
breaded veal cutlet, flavoured with cheese (Lombardy)

farsumagru palermitano
(fahrsoo**mar**groo pahlayrmee-**tar**noa)
braised meat with chopped hard-boiled eggs (Sicily)

fegato alla veneziana
(**fay**gahtoa **ahl**lah vaynayt**seear**nah)
thin slices of calf's liver fried with onions (Venice)

gulash
(**goo**lash)
chunks of beef stewed in paprika sauce

involtini
(eenvoal**tee**nee)
chicken-liver balls cooked in beef stock (Emilia-Romagna)

ossi buchi
(**oss**see **boo**kee)
veal knuckle and rice braised and served in a highly flavoured sauce (Lombardy)

saltimbocca alla romana
(sahlteem**boak**kah **ahl**lah roa**mar**nah)
escalope of veal braised in marsala wine with ham and sage (Latium)

scaloppina alla Val d'Aosta
(skahloa**pee**nah **ahl**lah vahl da**hos**tah)
veal scallop filled with cheese and ham

trippe alla fiorentina
(**treep**pay **ahl**lah feeorayn**tee**nah)
tripe and beef braised in a tomato sauce, served with cheese (Tuscany)

How do you like your meat?

baked	**al forno**	ahl **for**noa
barbecued	**alla graticola**	**ahl**lah grahtee**koa**lah
boiled	**lesso**	**lays**soa
braised	**brasato**	brah**ssar**toa
broiled	**allo spiedo**	**ahl**loa spee**ehd**oa
en casserole	**in casseruola**	een kass**sayroo**olah
fried	**fritto**	**freet**toa
grilled	**ai ferri**	ahee **fehr**ree
roasted	**arrostito**	ahr**roas**teetoa
stewed	**in umido**	een **oomee**doa
stuffed	**farcito**	fahr**cheet**oa
underdone (rare)	**al sangue**	ahl **sahng**gooay
medium	**a puntino**	ah poon**teen**oa
well-done	**ben cotto**	bain **kott**oa

Game and fowl

Many small fowl not regarded as game in America or Britain are served as first or main courses in Italy. They're usually grilled or roasted. Among small fowl considered fair game for the gourmet palate are lark, plover, thrush and ortolan.

I'd like some game.	**Vorrei della cacciagione.**	vor**raiee day**llah kahtchah**joan**ay
What poultry dishes do you serve?	**Che piatti di pollame servite?**	kay pee**ahttee** dee poall**ar**may sayr**vee**tay
allodola	ahl**lo**doalah	lark
anatroccolo	ahnah**trokk**oaloa	duckling
anitra	ar**nee**trah	duck
beccaccia	bay**kkaht**chah	woodcock
beccaccino	bay**kkaht**cheenoa	snipe
camoscio	kah**mosh**oa	chamois
cappone	kah**ppoan**ay	capon
capretto	kah**prayt**toa	kid goat
capriolo	kah**pree**oloa	roebuck
cervo	**chehr**voa	deer
cinghiale	cheeng**gee**arlay	wild boar
coniglio	koa**neel**yoa	rabbit
fagiano	fah**jar**noa	pheasant
faraona	fahrah**oan**ah	guinea fowl

gallina	gahlleenah	stewing fowl
gallo cedrone	gahlloa chedroanay	grouse
lepre	laipray	hare
oca	okah	goose
ortolano	oartoalarnoa	ortolan
pernice	payrneechay	partridge
piccione	peetchoanay	pigeon
piviere	peeveeehray	plover
pollo	poalloa	chicken
pollo novello	poalloa noavehlloa	spring chicken
porcellino da latte	poarchaylleenoa dah lahttay	sucking pig
quaglia	kwahlyah	quail
selvaggina	saylvahdjeenah	venison
tacchino	tahkkeenoa	turkey
tordo	toardoa	thrush

Game and fowl dishes

capretto ripieno al forno
(kahp**rayt**toa reepeeaynoa ahl fornoa)
stuffed kid, oven-roasted (Apulia, Calabria)

palombacce allo spiedo
(pahloam**baht**chay ah**ll**oa speeeh**doa**)
wood pigeon, spit-roasted (Umbria)

polenta e uccelli
(poa**lehn**tah ay oot**cheh**llee)
various small birds roasted on a spit and served with a mush made from maize flour (cornmeal mush) (Lombardy)

polenta e coniglio
(poa**lehn**tah ay koa**nee**lyoa)
rabbit stew served with polenta (see immediately above) (Venice)

Some common sauces and preparations

pesto alla genovese
(**pay**stoa ah**ll**ah jaynoa**vays**say)
olive oil, basil, cheese, garlic and pine nuts

pommarola alla napoletana
(poam**mah**rolah ah**ll**ah napoa**lay**tarnah)
tomatoes

ragù alla bolognese
(rah**goo** ah**ll**ah boaloa**ñays**say)
minced beef, onions, tomatoes, oil and herbs

salsa alla milanese
(**sahl**sah ah**ll**ah meelah**nay**ssay)
onions, tomatoes, bacon, butter and olive oil

EATING OUT

Vegetables

barbabietole	bahrbahbeeehtoalay	beetroot
carciofi	kahrchofee	artichoke
carote	kahrawtay	carrots
cavolfiore	kahvoalfeeoaray	cauliflower
cavoli	karvoalee	cabbage
cavolini di Bruxelles	kahvoaleenee dee broossayl	brussels sprouts
ceci	chaychee	chick-peas
cetrioli	chaytreeolee	cucumbers
cetriolini	chaytreeoaleenee	gherkins
cicoria	cheekoreeah	endive (U.S. chicory)
cipolle	cheepollay	onions
fagioli	fahjoalee	beans
fagiolini	fahjoaleenee	green beans
fave	farvay	broad beans
finocchi	feenokkee	fennel
funghi	foonggee	mushrooms
indivia	eendeeveeah	chicory (U.S. endive)
insalata	eensahlartah	green salad
lattuga	lahttoogah	lettuce
lenticchie	laynteekkeeay	lentils
mais dolce	maheess doalchay	maize (corn)
melanzane	maylahntsarnay	eggplant
peperoni	paypayroanee	peppers, pimentos
piselli	peessehllee	peas
pomidoro	poameedawroa	tomatoes
porcini	poarcheenee	boletus mushrooms
porri	porree	leaks
primizia	preemeetseeah	spring (adj.)
rape	rarpay	turnips
ravanelli	rahvahnehllee	radishes
riso	reessoa	rice
sedano	sehdahnoa	celery
spinaci	speenarchee	spinach
tartufi	tahrtoofee	truffles
bianchi/neri	beeahngkee/nayree	white/black
topinamburo	toapeenahmbooroa	Jerusalem artichoke
verdura mista	vehrdoorah meestah	mixed vegetables
verza	vehrdzah	green cabbage
zucca	tsookkah	kind of pumpkin (squash)
zucchini	tsookkeenee	vegetable marrow (zucchini)

Cheese

Italy produces a great variety of cheeses, many of them little known outside the locality in which they're made. Cheese is a separate course in many Italian meals, preceding the dessert.

mild cheese	*bel paese, caciocavallo, fontina, mascarpone, mozzarella, parmigiano-reggiano* (which we call parmesan), *provatura, ragusano*
sharp cheese	*asiago, gorgonzola* (resembles Danish and French blue), *provolone*
unusual varieties	*asiago* (sometimes made of ewe's milk), *caciocavallo* (sometimes made of mare's milk), *mozzarella* (still produced with buffalo milk south of Naples), *pecorino* (any of a variety of tangy ewe's milk cheeses), *ricotta* (often made from ewe's milk)

Fruit

Fruit is generally served after the cheese.

Do you have fresh fruit?	**Avete della frutta fresca?**	ahvaytay dayllah froottah frayskah
I'd like a fresh fruit cocktail.	**Vorrei una scelta di frutta fresca.**	vorraiee oonah shayltah dee froottah frayskah

albicocca	ahlbeekokkah	apricot
ananas	ahnahnahss	pineapple
anguria	ahnggooreeah	watermelon
arancia	ahrahnchah	orange
cachi	karkee	persimmon
castagne	kahstarñay	chestnuts
cedro	chaydroa	lime
ciliege	cheeleeayjay	cherries
cocomero	koakoamayroa	watermelon
fichi	feekee	figs
fragole	frargoalay	strawberries
lamponi	lahmpoanee	raspberries
limone	leemoanay	lemon
mandarini	mahndahreenee	tangerines
mandorle	mahndoarlay	almonds
mela	maylah	apple
mirtilli	meerteellee	blueberries
more	moray	mulberries

noci	noachee	walnuts
nocciole	noatcholay	hazelnuts
pera	payrah	pear
pesca	pehskah	peach
pompelmo	poampaylmoa	grapefruit
prugna	prooñah	plum
prugna secca	prooñah saykkah	prune
ribes	reebayss	red currants
uva	oovah	grapes

Dessert

As you've probably realized by now, Italian food is filling and you may not feel like a heavy dessert. The Italians feel the same. Few Italian restaurants serve pie or puddings of the substantial sort that we're used to at home. As an alternative, try some of the delicious ice-cream (*gelato*—jay**lar**toa) for which Italy is renowned. A *granita* (grah**nee**tah) makes a refreshing close to a meal. This is made by pouring syrup, juice or coffee over a glass of chipped ice.

I'd like a dessert, please.	**Vorrei un dessert, per favore.**	vorraiee oon dayss**sehr** pair fahvo**a**ray
Something light, please.	**Qualcosa di leggero, per favore.**	kwahl**kaw**ssah dee layd**jai**roa pair fahvo**a**ray
Just a small portion.	**Solo una piccola porzione.**	soaloa oonah **peek**koalah portseeo**a**nay
Nothing more, thanks.	**Nient'altro, grazie.**	neeehntahltroa **grar**tseeay

If you aren't sure what to order, ask the waiter:

What do you have for dessert?	**Che dessert avete?**	kay dayss**sehr** ahvaytay
What do you recommend?	**Cosa consiglia?**	**kaw**ssah koanseelyah
budino	boodeenoa	pudding
cassata gelata	kahsssartah jaylartah	ice-cream with candied fruit (U.S. spumoni)
cassata siciliana	kahsssartah seecheelyannah	sponge cake garnished with sweet cream cheese, chocolate and candied fruit

crema	kraimah	custard
dolce	doalchay	cake
gelato	jaylartoa	ice-cream
all'amarena	ahll ahmahraynah	wild-cherry
alla fragola	ahllah frargoalah	strawberry
al limone	ahl leemoanay	lemon
alla vaniglia	ahllah vahneelyah	vanilla
panforte di Siena	pahnfortay dee seeehnah	cake with candied fruit, cloves and pimento
panicielli d'uva passula	pahneechayllee doovah pahsssoolah	raisins wrapped in lemon leaves

That's the end of our Italian menu. For wine and other drinks, see the next pages. But after the feast comes...

The bill (check)

I'd like to pay.	**Vorrei pagare.**	vorraiee pahgarray
We'd like to pay separately.	**Vorremmo pagare separatamente.**	vorrehmmoa pahgarray saypahrahtahmayntay
You've made a mistake in this bill, I think.	**Penso che abbiate fatto un errore nel conto.**	pehnsoa kay ahbbeeartay fahttoa oon ayrroaray nayl koantoa
Is service included?	**È compreso il servizio?**	ai koamprayssoa eel sayrveetseeoa
Is everything included?	**È tutto compreso?**	ai toottoa koamprayssoa
Do you accept traveller's cheques?	**Accettate i traveller's cheques?**	ahtchayttartay ee "traveller's cheques"
Thank you, this is for you.	**Grazie, questo è per lei.**	grartseeay kooaystoa ai pair lehee
Keep the change.	**Tenga il resto.**	taynggah eel rehstoa
That was a very good meal.	**È stato un pasto molto buono.**	ai startoa oon parstoa moaltoa bwonoa
We enjoyed it, thank you.	**Ci è piaciuto grazie.**	chee ai peeahchootoa grartseeay

EATING OUT

SERVIZIO COMPRESO
SERVICE INCLUDED

Complaints

But perhaps you'll have something to complain about:

That's not what I ordered. I asked for...	**Non è ciò che avevo ordinato. Ho chiesto...**	noan ai cho kay ahvayvoa oardeenartoa. oa keeehstoa
May I change this?	**Posso cambiare questo?**	posssoa kahmbeearray kooaystoa
The meat is...	**La carne è...**	lah kahrnay ai
overdone	**troppo cotta**	troppoa kottah
underdone	**poco cotta**	pokoa kottah
too rare	**troppo al sangue**	troppoa ahl sahnggooay
too tough	**troppo dura**	troppoa doorah
This is too...	**Questo è troppo...**	kooaystoa ai troppoa
bitter / salty	**amaro / salato**	ahmarroa / sahlartoa
sweet	**dolce**	doalchay
The food is cold.	**Il cibo è freddo.**	eel cheeboa ai frayddoa
This isn't fresh.	**Questo non è fresco.**	kooaystoa noan ai frayskoa
What's taking you so long?	**Perchè avete impiegato tanto tempo?**	pehrkai ahvaytay eempeeaygartoa tahntoa tehmpoa
Where are our drinks?	**Dove sono le nostre bevande?**	doavay soanoa lay nostray bayvahnday
This isn't clean.	**Questo non è pulito.**	kooaystoa noan ai pooleetoa
Would you ask the head waiter to come over?	**Vuole chiedere al capo cameriere di venire qui?**	vwolay keeaydayray ahl karpoa kahmayreeehray dee vayneeray kooee

Drinks
Aperitifs

The average Italian is just as fond of his favourite *aperitivo* (ahpehree**tee**voa) as we are of our cocktail or highball. Often bittersweet, some aperitifs have a wine and brandy base with herbs and bitters while others may have a vegetable base. Here are some aperitifs you may want to try:

Americano (ahmayree**kar**noa)	despite its name, the most popular Italian aperitif; a vermouth to which bitters, brandy and lemon peel are added

Aperol (ahpayroal)	a non-alcoholic bitters	
Campari (kahm**par**ee)	reddish-brown bitters, flavoured with orange peel and herbs, it has a quinine taste	
Cynar... (cheenarr)	produced from artichoke	
Martini (mahrtee**nee**)	a brand-name vermouth not to be confused with a martini cocktail	
I'd like a Cynar...	**Vorrei un Cynar . . .**	vorrai**e** oon chee**narr**
neat (straight)	**liscio**	**lee**shoa
on the rocks	**con ghiaccio**	koan gee**aht**choa
with (seltzer) water	**con acqua (di seltz)**	koan ahk**kwah** (dee se**hltz**)

Wine

Italy produces nearly 2 thousand million gallons of wine annually and is thus the world's most important wine-producing country in terms of quantity. Vineyards are found all over the Italian peninsula and islands.

Some restaurants list their wines in a corner of the menu while others have them marked up on the wall. As much of the nation's wine doesn't travel well, don't expect a *trattoria* to offer more than a few types of wine. Most of the wine must be drunk young so don't look too hard for vintage labels. Wine—even red—is always served chilled in Italy.

Some of the country's most reputed wines (like *Barbaresco* and *Barolo*) comes from the Piedmont in northwestern Italy. But most other regions have noted wine, too. This is your opportunity to sample local wine, some of which is of surprisingly good quality.

Chianti is doubtless Italy's best-known wine outside of its borders. The best of it is produced between Florence and Siena. The term *chianti classico* on the label indicates that the production of this wine has been carefully supervised. A chianti of superior quality carries the term *riserva* on the label.

If you need help in choosing a wine, don't hesitate to ask the waiter. He'll often suggest a bottle of local renown.

Italians drink red wine with almost everything. But white wine is reserved for fish and seafood. However, if you're around the Lake of Garda, it's traditional to drink the light red *Bardolino* or *Valpolicella* with lake trout. A good rosé goes well with almost anything. The chart on the following page will help you to choose your wine if you want to do some serious wine-tasting.

I'd like...of...	Vorrei...di...	vorraiee...dee
a carafe	**una caraffa**	oonah kahrahffah
a bottle	**una bottiglia**	oonah botteelyah
half a bottle	**mezza bottiglia**	mehdzah botteelyah
a glass	**un bicchiere**	oon beekkeeairay
a litre	**un litro**	oon leetroa
I want a bottle of white/red wine.	**Vorrei una bottiglia di vino bianco/rosso.**	vorraiee oonah botteelyah dee veenoa beeahngkoa/roasssoa

dry	**secco**	sehkkoa
full-bodied	**pieno**	peeaynoa
light	**leggero**	laydjairoa
red	**rosso**	roasssoa
rosé	**rosatello**	rawzahtehlloa
sparkling	**spumante**	spoomahntay
sweet	**dolce**	doalchay
white	**bianco**	beeahngkoa

If you have enjoyed the wine, you may want to say:

Please bring me another...	**Per favore, mi porti...**	pair fahvoaray mee portee
glass	**un altro bicchiere**	oon ahltroa beekkeeairay
carafe	**un'altra caraffa**	oonahltrah kahrahffah
bottle	**un'altra bottiglia**	oonahltrah botteelyah
Where does this wine come from?	**Da dove viene questo vino?**	dah doavay veeaynay kooaystoa veenoa

Type of wine	Examples	Accompanies
sweet white wine	*Orvieto* from Umbria (the export variety is usually dry), *Aleatico* and *Vino Santo* from Tuscany and the famed *Marsala* from Sicily	desserts, especially custard, pudding, cake
dry white wine	*Frascati* from Latium or *Verdicchio dei Castelli di Jesi* from the Adriatic Marches; local white wine generally falls into this category	fish, seafood, cold or boiled meat, fowl (the unconventional Romans enjoy drinking *Frascati* with a heavy meal)
rosé	*Lagrein* from Trentino-Alto Adige	goes with most anything but especially cold dishes, eggs, pork and lamb
light-bodied red wine	*Bardolino* and *Valpoli-cella* from the Lake of Garda; local red wine, including Italian-Swiss *Merlot*, usually fits this category	roast chicken, turkey, veal, lamb, steaks, ham, liver, quail, pheasant, soft-textured cheeses, stews and pasta
full-bodied red wine	*Barolo* and *Barbaresco* from Piedmont	duck, goose, kidneys, most game, tangy cheese like *gorgonzola*—in short, any strong-flavoured dishes
sparkling white wine	*Asti spumante* (Italians like to refer to it as champagne but it's slightly sweet)	goes nicely with dessert and pastry; if it's dry, you might try *spumante* as an aperitif or with shellfish, nuts or dried fruit

EATING OUT

Other alcoholic drinks

Coffee shops and bars usually have a good stock of foreign and domestic beer, wine and liquor—even some of your favourite brands. Don't bother asking for any fancy cocktails or highballs except in the more sophisticated establishments or where signs are displayed saying *American bar*. Though not particularly noted for its beer, Italy does produce a number of local brews, especially in the North, which you might like to sample.

aperitif	**un aperitivo**	oon ahpayree**tee**voa
beer	**una birra**	**oo**nah **beer**rah
Bourbon	**un Bourbon**	oon "bourbon"
brandy	**un brandy**	oon "brandy"
cider	**del sidro**	dayl **seed**roa
cognac	**un cognac**	oon koa**ñahk**
cordial (Am.)	**un liquore**	oon leek**woa**ray
gin	**un gin**	oon "gin"
gin-fizz	**un gin-fizz**	oon "gin-fizz"
gin and tonic	**un gin e tonico**	oon "gin" ay to**nee**koa
liqueur	**un liquore**	oon leek**woa**ray
port	**un porto**	oon **por**toa
rum	**un rum**	oon room
Scotch	**uno Scotch**	**oo**noa "scotch"
sherry	**uno sherry**	**oo**noa "sherry"
vermouth	**un vermouth**	oon **vehr**moot
vodka	**della vodka**	**dayl**lah **vod**kah
whisky	**un whisky**	oon "whisky"
whisky and soda	**whisky e soda**	"whisky" ay **so**dah

glass	**un bicchiere**	oon beekkee**air**ay
bottle	**una bottiglia**	**oo**nah bot**teel**yah
double (a double shot)	**doppio**	**doap**peeoa
neat (straight)	**liscio**	**lee**shoa
on the rocks	**con ghiaccio**	kon gee**aht**choa

You'll certainly want to take the occasion to sip an after-dinner drink. If you'd like something which approaches French cognac try *Vecchia Romagna*. If you feel a digestive is called for, a glass of *Fernet-Branca* should fit the bill.

I'd like to try a glass of…, please.	**Vorrei assaggiare un bicchiere di…, per favore.**	vorraiee ahsssahdjarray oon beekkeeairay dee… pair fahvoaray
Are there any local specialities?	**Avete specialità locali?**	ahvaytay spaychahleetah loakarlee
Please bring me a… of…	**Per favore, mi porti un…di…**	pair fahvoaray mee portee oon…dee

CIN-CIN!
(cheen cheen)
CHEERS!

Soft drinks, coffee, tea

The Italian *caffè espresso* has a rich aroma and is excellent everywhere. Served in demi-tasses, it's stronger than what we're used to at home. However, if you'd like to try a more concentrated cup of espresso coffee, ask for a *ristretto* (reestrayttoa). As against this, a *caffè lungo* (kahffay loonggoa) is a slightly weaker cup of espresso coffee.

For breakfast don't miss the opportunity to drink a *cappuccino* (kahppootcheenoa), a delicious mixture of coffee and hot milk, dusted with cocoa. In summer, iced tea and coffee are popular.

I'd like a/an…	**Vorrei…**	vorraiee
chocolate	**un cioccolato**	oon choakkoalartoa
coffee	**un caffè**	oon kahffay
cup of coffee	**una tazza di caffè**	oonah tahttsah dee kahffay
coffee with cream	**un caffè con panna**	oon kahffay kon pahnnah
espresso coffee	**un caffè espresso**	oon kahffay aysprehsssoa
iced coffee	**un caffè freddo**	oon kahffay frayddoa
fruit juice	**un succo di frutta**	oon sookkoa dee froottah
grapefruit	**di pompelmo**	dee poampaylmoa
lemon	**di limone**	dee leemoanay
orange	**d'arancia**	dahrahnchah
pineapple	**d'ananas**	dahnahnahss
tomato	**di pomidoro**	poameedawroa
lemonade	**una limonata**	oonah leemoanartah

milk	**del latte**	dayl lahttay
milkshake	**un frullato di latte**	oon froollartoa dee lahttay
mineral water	**dell'acqua minerale**	dayllahkkwah meenayrarlay
orangeade	**un'aranciata**	oonahrahnchartah
soda water	**dell'acqua di seltz**	dayllahkkwah dee sehlts
squash (fruit drink)	**una spremuta**	oonah spraymootah
tea	**un tè**	oon tay
with milk / lemon	**con latte / limone**	kon láhttay/leemoanay
iced tea	**un tè freddo**	oon tay frayddoa
tonic water	**dell'acqua tonica**	dayllahkkwah toneekah

Eating light—Snacks

I'll have one of those, please.	**Per favore, vorrei uno di questi.**	pair fahvoaray vorraiee oonoa dee kooaystee
Give me two of these and one of those.	**Mi dia due di questi ed uno di quelli.**	mee deeah dooay dee kooaystee ayd oonoa dee kooayllee
to the left / right	**a sinistra / a destra**	ah seeneestrah/ah dehstrah
above / below	**sopra / sotto**	soaprah/soattoa
Please give me a / an / some...	**Per favore, mi dia...**	pair fahvoaray mee deeah
biscuits (Br.)	**dei biscotti**	daiee beeskottee
bread	**del pane**	dayl parnay
butter	**del burro**	dayl boorroa
cake	**della torta**	dayllah toartah
candy	**un dolce**	oon doalchee
(bar of) chocolate	**(una stecca di) cioccolata**	(oonah staykkah dee) choakkoalartah
cookies	**dei biscotti**	daiee beeskottee
hamburger	**un hamburger**	oon ahmboorgayr
hot-dog	**un hot dog**	oon "hot dog"
ice-cream	**un gelato**	oon jaylartoa
pastry	**dei dolci**	daiee doalchee
pie	**un pasticcio**	oon pahsteetchoa
roll	**un panino**	oon pahneenoa
salad	**un'insalata**	ooneensahlartah
sandwich	**un sandwich**	oon "sandwich"
sweets	**dei dolciumi**	daiee doalchoomee
toast	**un toast**	oon "toast"
waffles	**delle cialde**	dayllay chahlday
How much is that?	**Quant'è?**	kwahntai

Travelling around

Plane

Very brief—because at any airline office or airport you're sure to find someone who speaks English. But here are a few useful expressions you may want to know:

Do you speak English?	**Parla inglese?**	pahrlah eengglayssay
Is there a flight to Naples?	**C'è un volo per Napoli?**	chai oon voaloa pair narpoalee
Is it a nonstop flight?	**È un volo diretto?**	ai oon voaloa deerayttoa
When's the next plane to Palermo?	**A che ora parte il prossimo aereo per Palermo?**	ah kay oarah pahrtay eel prossseemoa ahairayoa pair pahlehrmoa
Do I have to change planes?	**Devo cambiare aereo?**	dayvoa kahmbeearray ahairayoa
Can I make a connection to Venice?	**Posso prendere una coincidenza per Venezia?**	posssoa prehndayray oonah koeencheedehntsah pair vaynaytseeah
I'd like a ticket to Milan.	**Vorrei un biglietto per Milano.**	vorraiee oon beelyayttoa pair meelarnoa
What's the fare to Torino?	**Quanto costa il biglietto per Torino?**	kwahntoa kostah eel beelyayttoa pair toareenoa
single (one-way)	**andata**	ahndartah
return (roundtrip)	**andata e ritorno**	ahndartah ay reetornoa
What time does the plane take off?	**A che ora decolla l'aereo?**	ah kay oarah daykollah lahairayoa
What time do I have to check in?	**Quanto tempo ho prima del controllo?**	kwahntoa tehmpoa oa preemah dayl koantrolloa
What's the flight number?	**Qual'è il numero del volo?**	kwahlai eel noomayroa dayl voaloa
What time do we arrive?	**A che ora arriveremo?**	ah kay oarah ahrreevayraymoa

ARRIVO	**PARTENZA**
ARRIVAL	DEPARTURE

Trains

If you are worried about railway tickets or time-tables, go to a travel agency where they speak English or see the *portiere* (poarteeayray) of your hotel.

Train travel in Italy is usually fast on the main lines. The trains (diesel and electric) run on time, although there may be delays during the tourist season. First-class coaches are comfortable: second-class, adequate.

Types of trains

TEE (teh-eh-eh)	A luxury, international service with first class only; additional fare and reservation required
Rapido (R.) (rarpeedoa)	Long-distance express luxury coaches; additional fare required
Direttissimo (D.D.) (deerehtteessseemoa)	Long-distance train, stopping at main stations
Diretto (D.) (deerehttoa)	Local train, stopping at the main stations
Accelerato (A.) (ahtchaylayrartoa)	Small local train, stopping at all stations
Locale (L.) (loakarlay)	Same as an *accelerato*

Here are some more useful terms which you may need.

Littorina (leettoareenah)	Small diesel used on short runs
Vagone letto (vahgonay lehttoa)	Sleeping-car with individual compartments and washing facilities
Carrozza cuccette (kahrrottsah kootchehttay)	A berth with blankets and pillows
Carrozza ristorante (kahrrotsah reestorahntay)	Dining-car
Bagagliaio (bahgahlyeeareeoa)	Guard's van (baggage car): normally only registered luggage permitted

To the railway station

Where's the railway station?	**Dove si trova la stazione ferroviaria?**	doavay see trawvah lah stahtseeoanay fehrrovee-arreeah
Taxi, please!	**Taxi, per favore!**	tahsssee pair fahvoaray
Take me to the railway station.	**Mi porti alla stazione ferroviaria.**	mee portee ahllah staht-seeoanay fehrroveearreeah
What's the fare?	**Quant'è?**	kwahntai

Where's the...?

Where is/are the...?	**Dove si trova...?**	doavay see trawvah
barber's shop	**il barbiere**	eel barbeeairay
booking office	**l'ufficio prenotazioni**	looffeecheeoa praynoatahtseeoanee
buffet	**il buffet**	eel booffay
currency-exchange office	**l'ufficio cambio**	looffeecheeoa **kahm**beeoa
information office	**l'ufficio informazioni**	looffeecheeoa eenfoarmahtseeoanee
left-luggage office (baggage check)	**il deposito bagagli**	eel daypozeetoa bahgahlyee
lost-property (lost-and-found) office	**l'ufficio oggetti smarriti**	looffeecheeoa odjehttee smahrreetee
luggage lockers	**la custodia automatica dei bagagli**	lah koostodeeah owtoamarteekah daiee bahgahlyee
news-stand	**l'edicola**	laydeekoalah
platform 7	**il binario 7**	eel beenarreeoa 7
reservations office	**l'ufficio prenotazioni**	looffeecheeoa praynoatahtseeoanee
restaurant	**il ristorante**	eel reestorahntay
snack bar	**lo "snack bar"**	loa "snack bar"
ticket office	**la biglietteria**	lah beelyayttayreeah
waiting-room	**la sala d'aspetto**	lah sarlah dahspehtto
Where are the toilets?	**Dove sono i gabinetti?**	doavay soanoa ee gahbeenayttee

INFORMAZIONI TURISTICHE	TOURIST INFORMATION
UFFICIO CAMBIO	CURRENCY EXCHANGE

FOR TAXI, see page 27

TRAVELLING AROUND

Inquiries

When is the...train to Rome?	Quando parte... treno per Roma?	kwahndoa pahrtay... traynoa pair roamah
first/last next	il primo/l'ultimo il prossimo	eel preemoa/loolteemoa eel prossseemoa
What time does the train for Milan leave?	A che ora parte il treno per Milano?	ah kay oarah pahrtay eel traynoa pair meelarnoa
What's the fare to Ancona?	Quanto costa il biglietto per Ancona?	kwahntoa kostah eel beelyeeehttoa pair ahngkoanah
Is it a through train?	È un treno diretto?	ai oon traynoa deerehttoa
Will the train leave on time?	Partirà in orario il treno?	pahrteerah een oararreeo eel traynoa
What time does the train arrive at Florence?	A che ora arriverà a Firenze il treno?	ah kay oarah ahrreevayrah ah feerehntsay eel traynoa
Is there a dining-car on the train?	C'è una carrozza ristorante sul treno?	chai oonah kahrrottsah reestorahntay sool traynoa
Is there a sleeping-car on the train?	C'è un vagone letto sul treno?	chai oon vahgonay lehttoa sool traynoa
Does the train stop at Lugano?	Il treno si fermerà a Lugano?	eel traynoa see fayrmayrah ah loogarnoa
What platform does the train for Verona leave from?	Da che binario parte il treno per Verona?	dah kay beenarreeoa pahrtay eel traynoa pair vayroanah
What platform does the train from Bari arrive at?	A che binario arriva il treno proveniente da Bari?	ah kay beenarreeoa ahrreevah eel traynoa provayneeehntay dah barree
I'd like to buy a time-table.	Vorrei comperare un orario ferroviario.	vorraiee koampayrarray oon oararreeoa fehrroveearreeoa

ENTRATA	ENTRANCE
USCITA	EXIT
AI BINARI	TO THE PLATFORMS

È un treno diretto.	It's a through train.
Deve cambiare a...	You have to change at...
Cambi a...e prenda un treno locale.	Change at...and get a local train.
Il binario 7 è...	Platform 7 is...
laggiù/su dalle scale a sinistra/a destra	over there/upstairs on the left/on the right
C'è un treno per... alle...	There's a train to... at...
Il suo treno partirà dal binario...	Your train will leave from platform...
Ci sarà un ritardo di... minuti.	There'll be a delay of... minutes.

Tickets

I want a ticket to Rome.	Desidero un biglietto per Roma.	dayzeedayroa oon beelyayttoa pair roamah
single (one-way)	andata	ahndartah
return (roundtrip)	andata e ritorno	ahndartah ay reetorrnoa
first class	prima classe	preemah klahsssay
Isn't it half price for the child?	Non si paga metà prezzo per il bambino?	noan see pargah maytah prehttsoa pair eel bahmbeenoa
He's/She's 13*.	Ha 13 anni*.	ah 13 ahnnee

Prima o seconda classe?	First or second class?
Andata o andata e ritorno?	Single or return (one-way or roundtrip)?
Quanti anni ha il bambino/ la bambina?	How old is he/she?

* In Italy children between 4 and 14 years of age pay half fare.

All aboard

Is this the right platform for the train to Bellinzona?	È il binario giusto per il treno che va a Bellinzona?	ai eel beenarreeoa joostoa pair eel traynoa kay vah ah behlleendzoanah
Is this the right train to Genoa?	È il treno giusto per Genova?	ai eel trayno joostoa pair jainoavah
Excuse me. May I get by?	Mi scusi. Posso passare?	mee skoozee. posssoa pahsssarray
Is this seat taken?	È occupato questo posto?	ai oakkoopartoa kooaystoa postoa

---

VIETATO FUMARE
NO SMOKING

I think that's my seat.	Penso che questo sia il mio posto.	paynsoa kay kooaystoa seeah eel meeoa postoa
Would you let me know before we get to Milan?	Può avvisarmi prima di arrivare a Milano?	pwo ahvveezarrmee preemah dee ahrreevahray ah meelarnoa
What station is this?	Che stazione è?	kay stahtseeoanay ai
How long does the train stop here?	Quanto tempo si ferma qui il treno?	kwahntoa tehmpoa see fayrmah kooee eel traynoa
When do we get to Pisa?	Quando arriveremo a Pisa?	kwahndoa ahrreevay-raymoa ah peezah

Sometime on the journey the ticket collector (*il controllore*— koantroalloaray) will come around and say: *Biglietti, per favore* (Tickets, please)!

Eating

If you want a full meal in the dining-car, you may have to get a ticket from the attendant who will come round to your compartment. There are usually two sittings for breakfast, lunch and dinner.

You can get snacks and drinks in the buffet-car and in the dining-car when it isn't being used for main meals. On some trains an attendant comes around with snacks, tea, coffee and soft drinks. At the larger stations there are refreshment carts.

| First/Second call for dinner. | Prima/Seconda chiamata per la cena. | preemah/saykoandah keearmartah pair lah chainah |
| Where's the dining-car? | Dov'è la carrozza ristorante? | doavai lah kahrrottsah reestorahntay |

Sleeping

Are there any free compartments in the sleeping-car?	Ci sono degli scompartimenti liberi nel vagone letto?	chee soanoa dailyee skoampahrteemayntee leebayree nail vargonay lehttoa
Where's the sleeping-car?	Dov'è il vagone letto?	doavai eel vahgonay lehttoa
Where's my berth?	Dov'è la mia cuccetta?	doavai lah meeah kootchehttah
Compartments 18 and 19, please.	Gli scompartimenti 18 e 19, per favore.	lyee skoampahrteemayntee 18 eh 19 pair fahvoaray
I'd like a lower berth.	Vorrei la cuccetta inferiore.	vorraiee lah kootchettah eenfayreeoray
Would you make up our berths?	Può preparare le nostre cuccette?	pwo praypahrarray lay nostray kootchehttay
Would you call me at 7 o'clock?	Può svegliarmi alle 7?	pwo svaylyarmee ahllay 7
Would you bring me some coffee in the morning?	Può portarmi un caffè domani mattina?	pwo portahrmee oon kahffai doamarnee mahtteenah

Baggage and porters

Porter!	Facchino!	fahkkeenoa
Can you help me with my bags?	Può prendere le mie borse?	pwo prehndayray lay meeay borsay
Please put them down here.	Per favore, le metta laggiù.	pair fahvoaray lay mayttah lahdjoo

Note: If you want to put them in the guard's van (baggage car), you should register them 24 hours in advance.

FOR PORTERS, also see page 24

TRAVELLING AROUND

Lost!

We hope you'll have no need for the following phrases on your trip... but just in case:

Where's the lost-property (lost- and-found) office?	Dove si trova l'ufficio oggetti smarriti?	doavay see trawvah loof-feecheeoa odjehttee smahrreetee
I've lost...	Ho perso...	oa pehrsoa
this morning yesterday	questa mattina ieri	kooaystah mahtteenah eeairee
I lost it in...	L'ho perso in...	loa pehrsoa een
It's very valuable.	È di molto valore.	ai dee moaltoa vahloaray

Underground (subway)

The *metropolitana* in Rome and Milan corresponds to the London underground or the New York subway. A map showing the various lines and stations is displayed outside every station and in every train compartment. The stations are indicated outside by a red M.

The fare is always the same, irrespective of the distance you travel. The *metropolitana* runs from 5.30 a.m. to 12.30 a.m.

Where's the nearest underground station?	Dove si trova la più vicina stazione della metropolitana?	doavay see trawvah lah peeoo veecheenah stahtseeoanay dayllah maytroapoaleetarnah
Does this train go to...?	Questo treno va a...?	kooaystoa traynoa vah ah
Where do I change for...?	Dove cambio per andare a...?	doavay kahmbeeoa pair ahndarray ah
Is the next station...?	La prossima stazione è...?	lah prossseemah stahtseeoanay ai

Bus – Tram (streetcar)

In most buses you pay as you enter. On some rural buses, you may find the driver also acting as the conductor. In Rome and other big cities you can buy a booklet of tickets for regular journeys.

I'd like a booklet of tickets.	Vorrei un blocchetto di biglietti.	vorraiee oon blokkehttoa dee beelyayttee
Where can I get a bus to the Vatican?	Dove posso prendere l'autobus per andare al Vaticano?	doavay posssoa prehndayray lowtoabooss pair ahndarray ahl vahteekarnoa
What bus do I take for the Colosseum?	Quale autobus devo prendere per andare al Colosseo?	kwarlay owtoabooss dayvoa prehndayray pair ahndarray ahl koaloasssaioa
Where's the...?	Dove si trova...?	doavay see trawvah
bus stop	la fermata d'autobus	lah fehrmartah dowtoabooss
terminus	il capolinea	eel kahpoleenayah
When is the...bus to the Lido?	A che ora parte... autobus per il Lido?	ah kay oarah pahrtay... owtoabooss pair eel leedoa
first/last next	il primo/l'ultimo il prossimo	eel preemoa/loolteemoa eel prossseemoa
How often do the buses to Trastevere run?	Ogni quanto tempo passano gli autobus per Trastevere?	oñee kwahntoa tehmpoa pahsssahnoa lyee owtoabooss pair trahstaivayray
How much is the fare to...?	Quanto costa il biglietto per...?	kwahntoa kostah eel beelyayttoa pair
Do I have to change buses?	Devo cambiare autobus?	dayvoa kahmbeearray owtoabooss
How long does the journey take?	Quanto tempo dura il percorso?	kwahntoa tehmpoa doorah eel payrkoarsoa
Will you tell me when to get off?	Può dirmi quando devo scendere?	pwo deermee kwahndoa dayvoa shayndayray

FERMATA D'AUTOBUS	REGULAR BUS STOP
FERMATA A RICHIESTA	STOPS ON REQUEST

I want to get off at the university.	**Desidero scendere all'università.**	dayzeedayroa **shayn**dayray ahllooneevayrsee**tah**
Please let me off at the next stop.	**Per favore, mi faccia scendere alla prossima fermata.**	pair fahvoaray mee **faht**cheeah **shayn**dayray ahllah prossseemah fehrmartah
May I please have my luggage?	**Per favore, mi può dare il mio bagaglio?**	pair fahvoaray mee pwo darray eel meeoa bahgarlyeeoa

There are fast long-distance buses which link major cities throughout Italy as well as bus service to out-of-the-way rural areas. You can adapt the phrases in the train section (pages 66–70) to bus travel.

Other means of transport

If you want to visit the Italian islands of Capri, Sardinia or Sicily, you'll find frequent boat service available from the mainland.

Or try one of these to get around:

bicycle	**la bicicletta**	lah beecheeclehttah
boat	**il battello**	eel bahttehlloa
houseboat	**la "casa galleggiante"**	lah karssah gahllaydjeeahntay
motorboat	**il motoscafo**	eel moatoaskarfoa
rowing-boat	**la barca a remi**	lah bahrkah ah raimee
sailing-boat	**la barca a vela**	lah bahrkah ah vaylah
helicopter	**l'elicottero**	layleekottayroa
hitch-hiking	**l'autostop**	lowtaostop
horseback riding	**cavalcare**	kahvahlkarray
hovercraft	**il battello su cuscini**	eel bahttehlloa soo koosheenee
moped (motor-bike)	**la motoretta**	lah moatoarehttah
motorcycle	**la motocicletta**	lah moatoacheeclehttah

and if you're really stuck, go...

walking	**a piedi**	ah peeaydee

Around and about – Sightseeing

Here we're more concerned with the cultural aspect of life than with entertainment; and, for the moment, with towns rather than the countryside. If you want a guide book, ask…

Can you recommend a good guide book for…?	Può consigliarmi una buona guida per…?	pwo konseelyahrmee oonah bwawnah gooeedah pair
Is there a tourist office?	C'è un ufficio turistico?	chai looffeecheeoa tooreesteekoa
Where's the tourist office/information centre?	Dov'è l'ufficio turistico/l'ufficio informazioni?	doavai looffeecheeoa tooreesteekoa/looffeecheeoa eenfoarmartseeoanee
What are the main points of interest?	Quali sono i principali punti di interesse?	kwahlee soanoa ee preencheeparlee poontee dee eentayraysssay
We're here for…	Siamo qui per…	seearmoa kooee pair
only a few hours	alcune ore soltanto	ahlkoonay oaray soltahntoa
a day	un giorno	oon joarnoa
three days	tre giorni	tray joarnee
a week	una settimana	oonah saytteemarnah
Can you recommend a sightseeing tour?	Può consigliarmi un giro turistico?	pwo konseelyahrmee oon jeeroa tooreesteekoa
Where does the bus start from?	Da dove parte l'autobus?	dah doavay pahrtay lowtoabooss
Will it pick us up at the hotel?	Passerà a prenderci all'albergo?	pahsssayrah ah prehndayrchee ahllahlbayrgoa
How much does the tour cost?	Quanto costa l'escursione?	kwahntoa kostah layskoorseeoanay
What time does the tour start?	A che ora si parte per l'escursione?	ah kay oarah see pahrtay pair layskoorseeoanay
What bus/tram (street-car) do we take?	Quale autobus/tram prendiamo?	kwahlay owtoabooss/trahm prehndeearmoa
We'd like to rent a car for the day.	Desideriamo noleggiare un'auto per tutto il giorno.	dayzeedayreearmoa noalaydjeearray oonowtoa pair toottoa eel joarnoa

FOR TIME OF DAY, see page 178

Is there an English-speaking guide?	C'è un cicerone che parla inglese?	chai oon cheechayroanay kay pahrlah eengglayssay
Where is/Where are the...?	Dove si trova/Dove si trovano...?	doavay see trawvah/ doavay see troavahnoa
abbey	l'abbazia	lahbbahtseeah
aquarium	l'acquario	lahkkwarreeoa
amphitheatre	l'anfiteatro	lahnfeetayartroa
art gallery	la galleria d'arte	lah gahllayreeah dahrtay
artists' quarter	il quartiere degli artisti	eel kwahrteeayray daylyee ahrteestee
botanical gardens	i giardini botanici	ee jahrdeenee botarneechee
building	l'edificio	laydeefeetchoa
business district	il quartiere degli affari	eel kwahrteeayray daylyee ahffarree
castle	il castello	eel kahstehlloa
catacombs	le catacombe	lay kartarkombay
cathedral	la cattedrale	lah kahttaydrarlay
cemetery	il cimitero	eel cheemeetairoa
city centre	il centro città	eel chayntroa cheettah
city hall	il municipio	eel mooneecheepeeoa
church	la chiesa	lah keeayzah
coliseum	il colosseo	eel koaloasssayoa
concert hall	la sala dei concerti	lah sarlah daiee konchehrtee
convent	il convento	eel konvayntoa
court house	il palazzo di giustizia	eel parlahttsoa dee joosteetseeah
downtown area	il centro città	eel chayntroa cheettah
fortress	la fortezza	lah fortehttsah
fountain	la fontana	lah foantarnah
gardens	i giardini	ee jahrdeenee
grotto	la grotta	lah grottah
harbour	il porto	eel portoa
library	la biblioteca	lah beebleeotaikah
market	il mercato	eel mayrkartoa
memorial	il memoriale	eel maymoareearlay
monastery	il monastero	eel moanahstairoa
monument	il monumento	eel moanoomayntoa
museum	il museo	eel moozaioa
old city	la città vecchia	lah cheettah vehkkeeah
opera house	il teatro dell'opera	eel tayartroa daylloapehrah
palace	il palazzo	eel pahlahttsoa
park	il parco	eel pahrkoa
parliament building	il palazzo del Parlamento	eel pahlahttsoa dayl pahrlarmayntoa

planetarium	il planetario	eel plahnaytarreeoa
presidential palace	il palazzo presi- denziale	eel pahlahttsoa prayssee- dayntseearlay
ruins	le rovine	lay roveenay
shopping centre	la zona degli acquisti	lah dzonah daylyee ahkkooeestee
shrine	il reliquario	eel rayleekwahreeoa
stadium	lo stadio	loa stardeeoa
statue	la statua	lah startooah
stock exchange	la borsa valori	lah borsah vahloaree
supreme court	la Corte Suprema	lah koartay soopraymah
synagogue	la sinagoga	lah seenahgogah
temple	il tempio	eel tehmpeeoa
tomb	la tomba	lah toambah
tower	la torre	lah toarray
university	l'università	looneevayrseetah
vaults	i sotterranei/le cripte	ee soattayrrarnayee/lay creeptay
zoo	lo zoo	loa dzoaoa

Admission

Is...open on Sundays?	È aperto la domenica il...?	ai ahpehrtoa lah doamay- neekah eel
When does it open?	Quando apre?	kwahndoa arpray
When does it close?	Quando chiude?	kwahndoa keeooday
How much is the entrance fee?	Quanto costa l'entrata?	kwahntoa kostah layntrartah
Is there any reduction for...?	C'è una riduzione per...?	chai oonah reedootseeoanay pair
students children	gli studenti i bambini	lyee stoodayntee ee bahmbeenee
Have you a guide book (in English)?	Avete una guida (in inglese)?	ahvaytay oonah gooeedah (een eengglayssay)
Can I buy a catalogue?	Posso comperare un catalogo?	posssoa koampayrarray oon kahtarloagoa
Is it all right to take pictures?	È permesso fare delle fotografie?	ai pehrmaysssoa farray dayllay foatoagrahfeeay

> **ENTRATA LIBERA**   ADMISSION FREE
> **VIETATO FOTOGRAFARE**   NO CAMERAS ALLOWED

SIGHTSEEING

Who – What – When ?

What's that building ?	**Che cos'è quest'edi-ficio ?**	kay kossai kooaystaydee-feechoa
Who was the...?	**Chi è stato...?**	kee ai **star**toa
architect	**l'architetto**	lahrkee**teht**toa
artist	**l'artista**	lahr**tees**tah
painter	**il pittore**	eel peet**toa**ray
sculptor	**lo scultore**	loa skool**toa**ray
Who built it ?	**Chi lo costruì ?**	kee loa koast**rooe**e
Who painted that picture ?	**Chi dipinse questo quadro ?**	kee dee**peen**say kooay**stoa kwar**droa
When did he live ?	**Quando è vissuto ?**	**kwahn**doa ai vees**soo**toa
When was it built ?	**Quando fu costruito ?**	**kwahn**doa foo koast**rooee**toa
Where's the house where...lived ?	**Dove si trova la casa in cui visse...?**	**doa**vah see **trav**vah lah **kars**sah een **kooe**e **vees**say
We're interested in...	**Ci interessiamo di...**	chee eentay**rayss**seearmoa dee
antiques	**antichità**	ahnteekee**tah**
archaeology	**archeologia**	ahrkayoaloa**jee**ah
art	**arte**	**ahr**tay
botany	**botanica**	bo**tar**neekah
ceramics	**ceramiche**	chay**rar**meekay
coins	**monete**	mo**nai**tay
crafts	**artigianato**	ahrteejar**nar**toa
fine arts	**belle arti**	**behl**lay **ahr**tee
furniture	**mobilio**	mo**beel**eeoa
geology	**geologia**	jayoaloa**jee**ah
history	**storia**	**stor**eeah
medicine	**medicina**	maydee**chee**nah
music	**musica**	**moo**zeekah
natural history	**storia naturale**	**stor**eeah nartoor**ar**lay
ornithology	**ornitologia**	oarneetoaloa**jee**ah
painting	**pittura**	peet**toor**ah
pottery	**terrecotte**	tehr**ray**kottay
prehistory	**preistoria**	praye**stor**eeah
sculpture	**scultura**	skool**toor**ah
wild life	**flora e fauna**	**flor**ah ay **far**oonah
zoology	**zoologia**	dzoaoaloa**jee**ah
Where's the... department ?	**Dov'è il reparto di/del...?**	doa**vai** eel ray**pahr**toa dee/dayl

Just the adjective you've been looking for...

It's...	È...	ai
amazing	**sorprendente**	soar**prayndehn**tay
awful	**spaventoso**	spah**vaynt**ossoa
beautiful	**bellissimo**	beh**lleess**seemoa
gloomy	**malinconico**	mahleeng**kon**eekoa
impressive	**impressionante**	eempraysssseeoa**nahn**tay
interesting	**interessante**	eentayrayss**sahn**tay
magnificent	**magnifico**	mah**ñee**feekoa
monumental	**monumentale**	moanoomayn**tar**lay
overwhelming	**opprimente**	oppree**mayn**tay
sinister	**sinistro**	see**nee**stroa
strange	**strano**	**strar**noa
superb	**superbo**	soo**pehr**boa
terrible	**terribile**	tayr**ree**beelay
terrifying	**terrificante**	tayrreefee**kahn**tay
tremendous	**tremendo**	tray**mehn**doa
ugly	**brutto**	**broot**toa

Religious services

Most churches and cathedrals are open to the public, except, of course, during mass.

Women should wear some form of head covering when entering a church; a scarf will do. Mini-skirts aren't permitted, nor are slacks, shorts and backless dresses.

Is there a/an...near here?	C'è una...qui vicino?	chai **oo**nah...**kooee vee**cheenoa
Catholic church	**chiesa cattolica**	kee**ay**zah kaht**toa**leekah
Protestant church	**chiesa protestante**	kee**ay**zah proatay**stahn**tay
synagogue	**sinagoga**	seenah**gog**ah
mosque	**moschea**	moa**skai**ah
At what time is...?	A che ora è...?	ah kay **oa**rah ai
mass	**la messa**	lah **mays**ssah
the service	**la funzione**	lah foontsee**oa**nay
Where can I find a ...who speaks English?	Dove posso trovare un...che parla inglese?	**doa**vay **poss**soa trawvar-ray oon...kay **pahr**lah eeng**glays**say
priest/minister	**prete/pastore**	**prai**tay/pahs**toa**ray
rabbi	**rabbino**	rahb**bee**noa

Relaxing

Cinema (movies) – Theatre

Cinema showings are usually continuous. The matinée usually starts around 2 p.m. There's generally an intermission midway through the feature film.

Theatres close one day a week but give matinées on Sundays. They start later than at home. Booking in advance is advisable.

You can find out what's playing from newspapers and billboards. In most large towns you'll find publications of the type "This Week in..."

Have you a copy of "This Week in..."?	Ha la rivista "Questa settimana in..."?	ah lah reeveestah kooaystah saytteemarnah een...
What's showing at the cinema tonight?	Cosa danno al cinema questa sera?	kawssah dahnnoa ahl cheenaymah kooaystah sayrah
What's playing at the...theatre?	Che spettacolo c'è al teatro...?	kay spayttarkoaloa chai ahl tayartroa
What sort of play is it?	Che genere di opera è?	kay jainayray dee opayrah ai
Who's it by?	Di chi è?	dee kee ai
Can you recommend (a)...?	Può consigliarmi...?	pwo konseelyahrmee
good film	un buon film	oon bwawn film
comedy	una commedia	oonah koammaideeah
something light	qualcosa di leggero	kwahlkawssah dee layd-jairoa
drama	un dramma	oon drahmmah
musical	un'operetta	oonopayrehttah
revue	una rivista	oonah reeveestah
thriller	un giallo	oon jahlloa
Western	un Western	oon western
At what theatre is that new play by... being performed?	In quale teatro vie-ne rappresentata la nuova opera teatrale di...?	een kwarlay tayartroa veeaynay rahpprayssayn-tartah lah nwawvah opayrah tayahtrarlay dee

Where's that new film by...being shown?	**Dov'è proiettato il nuovo film di...?**	doavai proaeeehttahtoa eel nooawvoa film dee
Who's in it?	**Chi sono gli attori?**	kee soanoa lyee ahttoaree
Who's playing the lead?	**Chi è l'attore principale?**	kee ai lahttoaray preen-cheeparlay
Who's the director?	**Chi è il regista?**	kee ai eel rayjeestah
What time does it begin?	**A che ora incomincia?**	ah kay oarah eengkoa-meencheeah
What time does the show end?	**A che ora termina lo spettacolo?**	ah kay oarah tehrmeenah loa spayttarkoaloa
What time does the first evening performance start?	**A che ora inizia il primo spettacolo serale?**	ah kay oarah eeneetseeah eel preemoa spayttarkoa-loa sayrarlay
Are there any tickets for tonight?	**Ci sono biglietti per questa sera?**	chee soanoa beelyayttee pair kooaystah sayrah
How much are the tickets?	**Quanto costano i biglietti?**	kwahntoa kostarnoa ee beelyayttee
I want to reserve 2 tickets for the show on Friday evening.	**Desidero prenotare 2 biglietti per lo spettacolo di venerdì sera.**	dayzeedayroa praynoatar-ray 2 beelyayttee pair loa spayttarkoaloa dee vaynayrdee sayrah
Can I have a ticket for the matinée on Tuesday?	**Posso avere un biglietto per lo spettacolo del pomeriggio di martedì?**	posssoa ahvayray oon beelyayttoa pair loa spayt-tarkoaloa dayl poamay-reedjoa dee mahrtaydee
I want a seat in the stalls (orchestra).	**Desidero una poltrona.**	dayzeedayroa oonah poaltroanah
Not too far back.	**Non troppo indietro.**	noan troppoa eendeeay-troa
Somewhere in the middle.	**A metà circa.**	ah maytah cheerkah
How much are the seats in the circle (mezzanine)?	**Quanto costano i posti in galleria?**	kwahntoa kostahnoa ee postee een gahllayreeah
May I please have a programme?	**Per favore, posso avere un programma?**	pair fahvoaray posssoa ahvayray oon programhmah
Can I check this coat?	**Posso depositare questo cappotto?**	posssoa daypoasseetarre kooaystoa kahppottoa

Sono spiacente, è tutto esaurito.	I'm sorry, we're sold out.
Vi sono solo alcuni posti in galleria.	There are only a few seats left in the circle (mezzanine).
Posso vedere il suo biglietto?*	May I see your ticket?*
Questo è il suo posto.	This is your seat.

Opera–Ballet–Concert

Where's the opera house?	**Dov'è il teatro dell'opera?**	doavai eel tayartroa dayllopayrah
Where's the concert hall?	**Dov'è la sala dei concerti?**	doavai lah sarlah daiee koanchehrtee
What's on at the opera tonight?	**Quale spettacolo c'è all'Opera questa sera?**	kwahlay spayttarkoaloa chai ahllopayrah kooaystah sayrah
Who's singing?	**Chi canta?**	kee kahntah
Who's dancing?	**Chi balla?**	kee bahllah
What time does the programme start?	**A che ora inizia il programma?**	ah kay oarah eeneetseeah eel programhmah
What orchestra is playing?	**Che orchestra suona?**	kay oarkaystrah sooonah
What are they playing?	**Cosa suonano?**	kawssah sooonahnoa
Who's the conductor?	**Chi è il maestro?**	kee ai eel mahehstroa

* It's customary at the theatre to give a small tip to the usherette after she has shown you to your seat.

Night-clubs

Rome has a good choice of top-notch night-clubs with the season running from October to mid-June. The smartest ones are located around the via Veneto. The swank clubs can be quite expensive but you'll find cozy, reasonably priced night spots in Rome as well as in other cities and resorts.

But find out the prices before you order—and allow for the various surcharges.

For most night-clubs a dark suit is sufficient.

Can you recommend a good night-club?	**Può consigliarmi un buon night-club?**	pwo konseelyahrmee oon bwawn "night-club"
Is there a floor show?	**C'è il varietà?**	chai eel vahreeaytah
What time does the floor show start?	**A che ora inizia il varietà?**	ah kay oarah eeneetseeah eel vahreeaytah
Is evening dress necessary?	**È necessario l'abito da sera?**	ai naychaysssarreeoa larbeetoa dah sayrah

And once inside...

A table for 2, please.	**Per favore, un tavolo per 2.**	pair fahvoaray oon tarvoaloa pair 2
My name's... I reserved a table for 4.	**Mi chiamo... Ho prenotato un tavolo per 4 persone.**	mee keearmoa...oa praynoatartoa oon tarvoaloa pair 4 payrsoanay
I telephoned you earlier.	**Ho telefonato.**	oa taylayfoanartoa
We haven't got a reservation.	**Non abbiamo la prenotazione.**	noan ahbbeearmoa lah praynoatahtseeoanay

Dancing

Where can we go dancing?	**Dove possiamo andare a ballare?**	doavay possseearmoa ahndarray ah bahllarray
Is there a discotheque in town?	**C'è una discoteca nella città?**	chai oonah deeskoataykah nayllah cheettah

There's a dance at the...	C'è un ballo al...	chai oon **bahl**loa ahl
Would you like to dance?	Vuole ballare?	**vwaw**lay bahl**lar**ray
May I have this dance?	Mi concede questo ballo?	mee koan**cheh**day koo**ays**toa **bahl**loa

Do you happen to play...?

On a rainy day, this page may solve your problems.

Do you happen to play chess?	Sa giocare a scacchi?	sah joa**kar**ray ah **skahk**kee
I'm afraid I don't.	No, mi dispiace.	noa mee deespee**ar**chay
No, but I'll give you a game of draughts (checkers).	No, ma posso fare una partita a dama.	noa mah **poss**soa **far**ray **oo**nah pahr**tee**tah ah **dar**mah
king	il re	eel ray
queen	la regina	lah ray**jee**nah
castle (rook)	la torre	lah **toar**ray
bishop	l'alfiere	lahlfee**ay**ray
knight	il cavallo	eel kah**vahl**loa
pawn	la pedina	lah pay**dee**nah
Checkmate!	Scacco matto!	**skahk**koa **maht**toa
Do you play cards?	Gioca a carte?	**joa**kah ah **kahr**tay
bridge	bridge	bridge
canasta	canasta	kar**nah**stah
gin rummy	ramino	rah**mee**noa
whist	whist	whist
pontoon (21)	tressette	trays**sait**tay
poker	poker	poker
ace	l'asso	**lahss**soa
king	il re	eel ray
queen	la regina	lah ray**jee**nah
jack	il fante	eel **fahn**tay
joker	la matta/il jolly	lah **maht**tah/eel jolly
hearts	cuori	**kwaw**ree
diamonds	quadri	**kwar**dree
clubs	fiori	fee**oa**ree
spades	picche	**peek**kay

Casino and gambling

Italy's casinos are all located in the northern part of the country—Campione near Como, the Lido near Venice, San Remo on the Italian Riviera and St. Vincent in the Aosta Valley.

To get into a casino, you'll need your passport. (You must be over 21.) You must also have a "clean record" in the gambling world. For your part, you need have no doubts about the honesty of the game. All legitimate casinos are strictly controlled and regularly inspected. Casinos are anxious to avoid any risk of scandal or adverse public relations.

The minimum stake is usually the equivalent of a halfdollar (U.S.) or four shillings. Entrance fees are nominal. The language of the casino is mostly French, but the croupiers will understand enough English for your requirements.

In addition there are horse and dog races where parimutuel bets are accepted. Italians play *totocalcio* with a passion. This is government-operated betting on the final scores of football games. Another popular game of chance is the weekly state lottery.

Sports

Italians love action sports like football (soccer) and motorcycle and speedboat racing. There are also horse shows, golf and tennis tournaments, water polo, trotting races and boating. For your own recreation you'll be able to go fishing, golfing, skin diving, swimming or play a round of tennis.

Where's the nearest golf course ?	**Dove si trova il campo da golf più vicino ?**	doavay see trawvah eel kahmpoa dah golf peeoo veecheenoa
Can we hire (rent) clubs ?	**Possiamo noleggiare le mazze ?**	possseearmoa noalayd-jarray lay mahttsay

RELAXING

Where are the tennis courts?	**Dove sono i campi de tennis?**	**doa**vay **soa**noa ee **kahm**pee dah tennis
Can I hire rackets?	**Posso noleggiare le racchette?**	**poss**soa noalaydjeearray lay rahk**keht**tay
What's the charge per...?	**Qual'è il prezzo per...?**	kwahlai eel **preht**tsoa pair
day/round/hour	**un giorno/una partita/un'ora**	oon **joar**noa/**oo**nah pahr**tee**tah/**oo**noarah
Where's the nearest race course (track)?	**Dov'è l'ippodromo più vicino?**	doa**vai** leep**poa**dromoa peeoo veecheenoa
What's the admission charge?	**Quanto costa l'entrata?**	**kwahn**toa kostah layntrartah
Is there a swimming pool here?	**C'è una piscina qui?**	chai **oo**nah pee**shee**nah kooee
Is it open-air or indoors?	**È una piscina all'aperto o coperta?**	ai **oo**nah pee**shee**nah ahllah**pehr**toa oa koa**pehr**tah
Is it heated?	**È riscaldata?**	ai reeskahl**dah**tah
Can one swim in the lake/river?	**Si può nuotare nel lago/fiume?**	see pwo nwaw**tar**ray nayl **lar**goa/fee**oo**omay
I'd like to see a boxing match.	**Vorrei vedere un incontro di pugilato.**	vor**rai**ee vay**day**ray oon eeng**koan**troa dee poojee**lar**toa
Can you get me a couple of tickets?	**Può procurarmi un paio di biglietti?**	pwo proakoo**rar**mee oon **par**eeoa dee beel**yayt**tee
Is there a football (soccer) match anywhere this Saturday?	**C'è una partita di calcio da qualche parte, sabato?**	chai **oo**nah pahr**tee**tah dee **kahl**choa dah **kwahl**kay **pahr**tay **sar**bahtoa
Who's playing?	**Chi gioca?**	kee **joa**kah
Is there any good fishing around here?	**Ci sono buone possibilità di pesca in questa zona?**	chee **soa**noa boo**aw**nay possseebeeleetah dee **pay**skah een koo**ay**stah **dzoa**nah
Do I need a permit?	**È necessario il permesso?**	ai naychayss**sar**reeoa eel pay**rmayss**soa
Where can I get one?	**Dove posso procurarmene uno?**	**doa**vay **poss**soa proakoo**rar**maynay **oo**noa

On the beach

Is it safe for swimming?	**Si può nuotare senza pericolo?**	see pwo nwawtarray sayntsah payreekoaloa
Is there a lifeguard?	**C'è un bagnino?**	chai oon bahñeenoa
Is it safe for children?	**È sicuro per i bambini?**	ai seekooroa pair ee bahmbeenee
There are some big waves.	**Ci sono cavalloni.**	chee soanoa kahvahlloanee
Are there any dangerous currents?	**Vi sono correnti pericolose?**	vee soanoa koarrayntee payreekoaloasay
What time is high tide?	**A che ora è l'alta marea?**	ah kay oarah ai lahltah marrayah
What time is low tide?	**A che ora è la bassa marea?**	ah kay oarah ai lah bahssah marrayah
What's the temperature of the water?	**Qual'è la temperatura dell'acqua?**	kwahlai lah taympayrahtoorah dayllahkkwah
I want to hire a/an...	**Vorrei noleggiare...**	vorraiee noalaydjarray
air mattress	**un materassino pneumatico**	oon mahtayrahsssseenoa pnayoomarteekoa
bathing hut	**una cabina**	oonah kahbeenah
deck-chair	**una sedia a sdraio**	oonah saydeeah ah sdrareeoa
skin-diving equipment	**un equipaggiamento subacqueo**	oon aykooeepahdjahmayntoa soobahkkooayoa
sunshade	**un ombrellone**	oon oambraylloanay
surf board	**un sandolino**	oon sahndoaleenoa
tent	**una tenda**	oonah taindah
some water-skis	**degli sci nautici**	daylyee shee nowteechee
Where can I rent a...?	**Dove posso noleggiare una...?**	doavay posssoa noalaydjarray oonah
canoe	**canoa**	kahnoah
motor-boat	**barca a motore**	bahrkah ah motoaray
rowing-boat	**barca a remi**	bahrkah ah raymee
sailing-boat	**barca a vela**	bahrkah ah vailah
What's the charge per hour?	**Quanto costa all'ora?**	kwahntoa kostah ahlloarah

RELAXING

SPIAGGIA PRIVATA PRIVATE BEACH	**VIETATO FARE IL BAGNO** NO BATHING

Winter sports

While one doesn't think of going skiing in sunny Italy, it is possible particularly in winter. There are a number of ski resorts in the Dolomite Alps and the Piedmont region in northern Italy. Surprisingly, one could also ski at Terminello, not far from Rome, or on Mount Aetna in Sicily.

Is there a skating-rink near here?	C'è una pista di pattinaggio qui vicino?	chai oonah peestah dee pahtteenadjoa kooee veecheenoa
I want to hire some skates.	Vorrei noleggiare dei pattini.	vorraiee noalaydjarray daiee pahtteenee
What are the skiing conditions like at Cortina d'Ampezzo?	Come sono le condizioni per sciare a Cortina d'Ampezzo?	koamay soanoa lay kondeetseeoanee pair sheearray ah koarteenah dahmpehttsoa
Can I take skiing lessons there?	Posso prendere delle lezioni di sci?	posssoa prehndarray dayllay laytseeoanee dee shee
Are there ski lifts?	Ci sono degli ski-lift?	chee soanoa daylyee ski-lift
I want to hire a/some...	Vorrei noleggiare...	vorraiee noalaydjarray
ice skates	dei pattini	daiee pahtteenee
skiing equipment	una tenuta da sci	oonah taynootah dah shee
toboggan	un toboga	oon tawboagah
sled	una slitta	oonah sleettah
boots	degli scarponi da sci	daylyee skahrpoanee dah shee
poles	dei bastoni	daiee bahstoanee
skis	degli sci	daylyee shee

Camping – Countryside

Camping isn't allowed without a permit in many parts of Italy. However, there are many authorised camping sites with excellent facilities. If you want to be on the safe side, go to one that's recognised by the Italian Tourist Association (TCI).

Can we camp here?	**Possiamo accamparci qui?**	posssee**ar**moa ahk**kahmpahr**chee kooee
Where can one camp for the night?	**Dove possiamo campeggiare questa notte?**	**doa**vay posssee**ar**moa kahm**payd**jarray kooaystah **not**tay
Is there a camping site near here?	**C'è una zona di campeggio qui vicino?**	chai oonah **dzoa**nah dee kahm**payd**joa kooee veecheenoa
May we camp in your field?	**Possiamo accamparci nel suo campo?**	posssee**ar**moa ahk**kahmpahr**chee nayl **soo**oa **kahm**poa
Can we park our caravan (trailer) here?	**Possiamo parcheggiare qui la nostra roulotte?**	posssee**ar**moa pahr**kaydjar**ray kooee lah **nos**trah roo**lot**
Is this an official camping site?	**È una zona di campeggio autorizzata?**	ai oonah **dzoa**nah dee kahm**payd**joa owtoareed-**dzar**tah
May we light a fire?	**Possiamo accendere un fuoco?**	posssee**ar**moa aht**chehn**-dayray oon **fwaw**koa
Is there drinking water?	**C'è acqua potabile?**	chai **ahk**kwah poatar-**bee**lay
What are the facilities?	**Quali sono le facilitazioni?**	**kwar**lee **soa**noa lay fahcheeleetartsee**oa**anee
Are there shopping facilities on the site?	**Ci sono possibilità d'acquisti sul posto?**	chee **soa**noa posssee**bee**-leetah dahk**kooees**tee sool **poas**toa
Are there...?	**Ci sono...?**	chee **soa**noa
baths	**i bagni**	ee **bar**ñee
showers	**le docce**	lay **dot**chay
toilets	**i gabinetti**	ee gahbee**nayt**tee

CAMPING

What's the charge...?	**Quanto si paga...?**	kwahntoa see pargah
per day	**al giorno**	ahl joarnoa
per person	**per persona**	pair payrsoanah
for a car	**per una macchina**	pair oonah mahkkeenah
for a tent	**per una tenda**	pair oonah taindah
for a caravan (trailer)	**per una roulotte**	pair oonah roolot
Is there a youth hostel near here?	**C'è un ostello della gioventù qui vicino?**	chai oon oastehlloa dayl- lah joavayntoo kooee veecheenoa
Do you know anyone who can put us up for the night?	**Conosce qualcuno che può alloggiarci per questa notte?**	koanoashay kwahlkoonoa kay pwo ahllodjahrchee pair kooaystah nottay

<table>
<tr><td>

VIETATO CAMPEGGIARE

NO CAMPING
</td><td>

ROULOTTE VIETATE

NO CARAVANS (TRAILERS)
</td></tr>
</table>

Landmarks

barn	**la baracca**	lah bahrahkkah
bridge	**il ponte**	eel poantay
brook	**il ruscello**	eel rooshehlloa
building	**l'edificio**	laydeefeecheeoa
canal	**il canale**	eel kahnarlay
church	**la chiesa**	lah keeaizah
cliff	**la scogliera**	lah skoalyayrah
copse	**il boschetto**	eel boaskehttoa
cornfield	**il campo di grano**	eel kahmpoa dee grarnoa
cottage	**il villino**	eel veelleenoa
crossroads	**l'incrocio**	leengkroachoa
farm	**la fattoria**	lah fahttoareeah
ferry	**il traghetto**	eel trahgehttoa
field	**il campo**	eel kahmpoa
footpath	**il sentiero**	eel saynteeayroa
forest	**la foresta**	lah fawrehstah
hamlet	**il gruppo di casolari**	eel grooppoa dee kahssoa- larree
heath	**la brughiera**	lah broogeeayrah
highway	**l'autostrada**	lowtoastrardah
hill	**la collina**	lah koalleenah
house	**la casa**	lah karssah
inn	**la locanda**	lah loakahndah
jungle	**la giungla**	lah joonglah
lake	**il lago**	eel largoa
marsh	**la palude**	lah pahlooday

CAMPING

moorland	la landa	lah lahndah
mountain	la montagna	lah moantarñah
mountain range	la catena di montagne	lah kahtaynah dee moantarñay
path	il viottolo	eel veeottoaloa
peak	il picco	eel peekkoa
plantation	la piantagione	lah peeahntahjoanay
pond	lo stagno	loa starñoa
pool	la piscina	lah peesheenah
railway	la ferrovia	lah fehrroaveeah
river	il fiume	eel feeoomay
road	la strada	lah strardah
sea	il mare	eel marray
spring	la sorgente	lah soarjayntay
stream	il torrente	eel toarrehntay
swamp	l'acquitrino	lahkkooeetreenoa
track	la pista	lah peestah
tree	l'albero	lahlbayroa
valley	la valle	lah vahllay
village	il villaggio	eel veellahdjeeoa
vineyard	la vigna	lah veeñah
water	l'acqua	lahkkwah
waterfall	la cascata	lah kahskartah
well	il pozzo	eel poąttsoa
wood	il bosco	eel boaskoa

CAMPING

VIETATO L'INGRESSO
NO TRESPASSING

What's the name of that river?	Come si chiama quel fiume?	koamay see keearmah kooayl feeoomay
How high is that mountain?	Quanto è alta quella montagna?	kwahntoa ai ahltah kooayllah moantarñah
Is there a scenic route to...?	C'è una strada panoramica per...?	chai oonah strardah pahnoararmeekah pair

...and if you're tired of walking, you can always try hitch-hiking—though you may have to wait a long time for a lift.

| Can you give me a lift to...? | Può darmi un passaggio fino a...? | pwo dahrmee oon pahsssahdjeeoa feenoa ah |

FOR ASKING THE WAY, see page 144

Making friends

Introductions

Here are a few phrases to get you started:

How do you do?	**Molto lieto.**	moaltoa leeaytoa
How are you?	**Come sta?**	koamay stah
Very well, thank you.	**Benissimo, grazie.**	baineessseemoa grartseeay
How's life?	**Come va?**	koamay vah
Fine, thanks. And you?	**Bene, grazie. E lei?**	bainay grartseeay. ay laiee
May I introduce Miss Philips?	**Posso presentarle la signorina Philips?**	posssoa prayzayntarrlay lah seeñoareenah Philips
I'd like you to meet a friend of mine.	**Vorrei che conoscesse un mio amico.**	vorraiee kay koanoashaysssay oon meeoa ahmeekoa
John, this is...	**John, ti presento...**	john tee prayzayntoa
My name's...	**Mi chiamo...**	mee keearmoa
Glad to know you.	**Lieto di fare la sua conoscenza.**	leeaytoa dee farray lah sooah koanoashehntsah

Follow-up

How long have you been here?	**Da quanto tempo è qui?**	dah kwahntoa tehmpoa ai kooee
We've been here a week.	**Siamo qui da una settimana.**	seearmoa kooee dah oonah saytteemarnah
Is this your first visit?	**È la prima volta che viene?**	ai lah preemah voltah kay veeaynay
No, we came here last year.	**No, siamo già venuti l'anno scorso.**	noa seearmoa jah vaynootee lahnnoa skoarsoa
Are you enjoying your stay?	**Le piace il suo soggiorno?**	lay peearchay eel soooa soadjoarnoa
Yes, I like...very much.	**Sì, ...mi piace molto.**	see...mee peearchay moaltoa
Are you on your own?	**È solo/sola?**	ai soaloa/soalah

I'm with...	Sono con...	soanoa kon
my wife	mia moglie	meeah moalyay
my husband	mio marito	meeoa mahreetoa
my family	la mia famiglia	lah meeah fahmeelyah
my parents	i miei genitori	ee meeehee jayneetoaree
some friends	degli amici	daylyee ahmeechee
Where do you come from?	Da dove viene?	dah doavay veeaynay
What part of...do you come from?	Da che parte della...viene?	dah kay pahrtay dayllah... veeaynay
I'm from...	Sono di...	soanoa dee
Where are you staying?	Dove soggiorna?	doavay soadjoarnah
I'm a student.	Sono studente.	soanoa stoodehntay
What are you studying?	Che cosa studia?	kay kawssah stoodeeah
We're here on holiday.	Siamo qui in vacanza.	seearmoa kooee een vahkahntsah
I'm here on a business trip.	Sono qui in viaggio d'affari.	soanoa kooee een veeahd-joa dahffarree
What kind of business are you in?	Di che genere d'affari si occupa?	dee kay jaynayray dahffar-ree see oakkoopah
I hope we'll see you again soon.	Spero di rivederla presto.	spayroa dee reevaydehrlah prehstoa
See you later.	A più tardi.	ah peeoo tahrdee
See you tomorrow.	A domani.	ah domarnee

The weather

They talk about the weather just as much in Italy as the British and Americans are supposed to do. So...

What a lovely day!	Che bella giornata!	kay behllah joarnartah
What awful weather.	Che tempo orribile.	kay tehmpoa oarreebeelay
Isn't it cold today?	Che freddo fa oggi, vero?	kay frehddoa fah odjee vehroa
Isn't it hot today?	Che caldo fa oggi, vero?	kay kahldoa fah odjee vehroa

Is it usually as warm as this?	Fa sempre caldo così?	fah **saympray kahl**doa kawssee
It's very foggy, isn't it?	È molto nebbioso, vero?	ai **moal**toa naybbeeoazoa **veh**roa
Do you think it'll... tomorrow?	Pensa che domani...?	**payn**sah kay domarnee
rain/snow	pioverà/nevicherà	peeovayrah/nayveekayrah
clear up	si schiarirà	see skeeahreerah
be sunny	ci sarà il sole	chee sahrah eel soalay

Invitations

My wife and I would like you to dine with us on...	Mia moglie ed io saremmo lieti di averla a cena da noi il...	meeah moalyay ayd eeoa sarrehmmoa leeaytee dee ahvayrlah ah chainah dah noaee eel
Can you come to dinner tomorrow night?	Viene a cena domani sera?	veeaynay ah chainah domarnee sayrah
We're giving a small party tomorrow night. I do hope you can come.	Faremo una festicciola domani sera. Spero veramente che possa venire.	fahraymoa oonah faysteetcholah domarnee sayrah. spayroa vayrahmayntay kay poasssah vayneeray
Can you come over for cocktails this evening?	Viene ad un cocktail questa sera?	veeaynay ahd oon cocktail kooaystah sayrah
There's a party. Are you coming?	C'è una festicciola. Viene?	chai oonah faysteetcholah. veeaynay
That's very kind of you.	È molto gentile da parte sua.	ai moaltoa jaynteelay dah pahrtay sooah
Great. I'd love to come.	Fantastico. Sarei lieto di venire.	fahntahsteekoa. sahrehee leeaytoa dee vayneeray
What time shall we come?	A che ora dobbiamo venire?	ah kay oarah doabbeearmoa vayneeray
May I bring a friend?	Posso portare un amico?	posssoa portarray oon ahmeekoa
May I bring my girl friend?	Posso portare la mia ragazza?	posssoa portarray lah meeah rahgahttsah

I'm afraid we've got to go now.	**Mi dispiace, ma adesso dobbiamo andare.**	mee deespeearchay mah ahdehsssoa doabbeearmoa ahndarray
Next time you must come to visit us.	**La prossima volta dovete venire da noi.**	lah prossseemah voltah doavaytay vayneeray dah noaee
Thanks for the evening. It was great.	**Grazie per la serata. È stata splendida.**	grartseeay pair la sayrartah. ai startah splehndeedah

Dating

Would you like a cigarette?	**Posso offrirle una sigaretta?**	posssoa offreerlay oonah seegahrayttah
Do you have a light, please?	**Ha un fiammifero, per favore?**	ah oon feeahmmeefayroa pair fahvoaray
Can I get you a drink?	**Posso offrirle qualcosa da bere?**	posssoa offreerlay kwahlkawssah dah bayray
Excuse me, could you please help me?	**Scusi, può aiutarmi?**	skoozee pwo ighootarrmee
I'm lost. Can you show me the way to…?	**Mi sono perduto. Può indicarmi la strada per…?**	mee soanoa pehrdootoa. pwo eendeekarrmee lah strardah pair
Are you waiting for someone?	**Aspetta qualcuno?**	ahspayttah kwahlkoonoa
Are you free this evening?	**È libera stasera?**	ai leebayrah stahssayrah
Would you like to go out with me tonight?	**Uscirebbe con me stasera?**	oosheerehbbay kon may stahssayrah
Would you like to go dancing?	**Le piacerebbe andare a ballare?**	lay peeahchayrehbbay ahndarray ah bahllarray
I know a good discotheque.	**Conosco una buona discoteca.**	koanoaskoa oonah bwawnah deeskoataykah
Shall we go to the cinema (movies)?	**Andiamo al cinema?**	ahndeearmoa ahl cheenaymah
Would you like to go for a drive?	**Andiamo a fare un giro in macchina?**	ahndeearmoa ah farray oon jeeroa een mahkkee-nah
Where shall we meet?	**Dove possiamo incontrarci?**	doavay possseearmoa eengkontrarrchee

I'll pick you up at your hotel.	**Passerò a prenderla all'albergo.**	pahsssayroa ah prayn-dayrlah ahllahlbehrgoa
I'll call for you at 8.	**Passerò da lei alle 8.**	pahsssayroa dal laiee ahllay 8
May I take you home?	**Posso accompagnarla a casa?**	posssoa ahkkoampahñarr-lah ah karssah
Can I see you again tomorrow?	**Posso rivederla domani?**	posssoa reevaydayrlah doamarnee
Thank you, it's been a wonderful evening.	**Grazie, è stata una magnifica serata.**	grartseeay ai startah oonah mahñeefeekah sayrartah
I've enjoyed myself tremendously.	**Mi sono divertito moltissimo.**	mee soanoa deevayrteetoa moalteessseemoa
What's your telephone number?	**Qual'è il suo numero di telefono?**	kwahlai eel soooa noo-mayroa dee taylaifoanoa
Do you live alone?	**Vive sola?**	veevay soalah
What time is your last train?	**A che ora parte il suo ultimo treno?**	ah kay oarah pahrtay eel soooa oolteemoa traynoa

Shopping guide

This shopping guide is designed to help you find what you want with ease, accuracy and speed. It features:

1. a list of all major shops, stores and services (p. 98)

2. some general expressions required when shopping to allow you to be specific and selective (p. 100)

3. full details of the shops and services most likely to concern you. Here you'll find advice, alphabetical lists of items and conversion charts listed under the headings below.

SHOPPING GUIDE

Shops, stores and services

If you have a pretty clear idea of what you want before you set out, then look under the appropriate heading, pick out the article and find a suitable description for it (colour, material, etc.).

Shop hours in Italy differ from summer to winter. In winter the shops are generally open from 8 a.m. to 7 p.m. with a lunch break between 1 and 3 p.m. During the tourist season, shops open and close later in the afternoon (4 to 8 p.m.).

Some remain open on Sundays but most close a half day during the week—often Monday morning or Thursday afternoon.

Swiss shops are open from 8 a.m. to noon or 12.30 p.m. and from 1.30 to 6.30 or 7 p.m. (Saturdays until 5 p.m.) with half-day closings similar to Italy.

Where's the nearest...?	Dove si trova... più vicino (vicina)?	doavay see trawvah... peeoo veecheenoa (veecheenah)
antique shop	l'antiquario	lahnteekwarreeoa
art gallery	la galleria d'arte	lah gahllayreeah dahrtay
baker's	la panetteria	lah pahnehttayreeah
bank	la banca	lah bahngkah
barber's	il barbiere	eel bahrbeeayray
beauty salon	l'istituto di bellezza	leesteetootoa dee behllehttsah
bookshop	la libreria	lah leebrayreeah
butcher's	la macelleria	lah mahchayllayreeah
chemist's	la farmacia	lah fahrmahcheeah
cobbler's	il calzolaio	eel kahltsoalareeoa
confectioner's	la pasticceria	lah pahsteetchayreeah
dairy	la latteria	lah lahttayreeah
delicatessen	la salumeria	lah sahloomayreeah
dentist	il dentista	eel daynteestah
department store	il grande magazzino	eel grahnday mahgahddzeenoa
doctor	il dottore	eel doattoaray
dressmaker's	la sartoria per signora	lah sahrtoareeah pair seeñoarah
drugstore	la farmacia	lah fahrmahcheeah

SHOPPING GUIDE

dry cleaner's	la tintoria	lah teentoareeah
fishmonger's	la pescheria	lah payskayreeah
furrier's	la pellicceria	lah paylleetchayreeah
greengrocer's	il negozio di frutta e verdura	eel naygotseeoa dee froottah ay vehrdoorah
grocery	la drogheria	lah drogayreeah
hairdresser's (ladies)	la parrucchiera	lah pahrrookkeeairah
hardware store	il negozio di ferramenta	eel naygotseeoa dee fehrrarmayntah
hospital	l'ospedale	lospaydarlay
jeweller's	la gioielleria	lah joaeeayllayreeah
launderette	la lavanderia automatica	lah lahvahndayreeah owtoamarteekah
laundry	la lavanderia	lah lahvahndayreeah
liquor store	il negozio di liquori	eel naygotseeoa dee leekwoaree
market	il mercato	eel mayrkartoa
newsagent's	il giornalaio	eel joarnahlareeoa
news-stand	l'edicola	laydeekoalah
optician	l'ottico	lotteekoa
photo shop	il negozio d'appa-recchi fotografici	eel naygotseeoa dahppah-rehkkee foatoagrarfee-chee
police station	il posto di polizia	eel poastoa dee poalee-tseeah
post office	l'ufficio postale	looffeechoa poastarlay
shoemaker's (repairs)	il calzolaio	eel kahltsoalareeoa
shoe shop	il negozio di scarpe	eel naygotseeoa dee skahrpay
souvenir shop	il negozio di ricordi	eel naygotseeoa dee reekordee
sporting goods shop	il negozio di articoli sportivi	eel naygotseeoa dee ahr-teekoalee sporteevee
stationer's	la cartoleria	lah kahrtoalayreeah
supermarket	il supermercato	eel soopairmayrkartoa
telegraph office	l'ufficio telegrafico	looffeechoa taylaygrar-feekoa
tobacconist's	la tabaccheria	lah tahbahkkayreeah
toy shop	il negozio di giocattoli	eel naygotseeoa dee joakahttoalee
travel agent	l'agenzia di viaggi	lahjayntseeah dee veeahdjee
wine merchant's	il vinaio	eel veenareeoa

SVENDITA   SALE

General expressions

Here are some expressions which will be useful to yo
when you're out shopping:

Where?

Where's a good...?	**Dov'è un buon...?**	doavai oon bwawn
Where's the nearest...?	**Dov'è il... più vicino?**	doavai eel... peeoo veecheenoa
Where can I find a...?	**Dove posso trovare un...?**	doavay posssoa trawvarray oon
Where's the main shopping area?	**Dov'è la zona principale dei negozi?**	doavai lah dzoanah preen- cheeparlay daïee naygotsee
How far is it from here?	**Quanto dista da qui?**	kwahntoa deestah dah kooee
How do I get there?	**Come ci si può arrivare?**	koamay chee see pwo ahrreevarray

Service

Can you help me?	**Può aiutarmi?**	pwo ighootarrmee
I'm just looking around.	**Do soltanto un'occhiata.**	doa soaltahntoa oonokkeeeartah
I want...	**Desidero...**	dayzeedayroa
Can you show me some...?	**Può mostrarmi dei...?**	pwo moastrarrmee daïee
Do you have any...?	**Ha dei...?**	ah daïee

That one

Can you show me...?	**Mi può mostrare...?**	mee pwo moastrarray
that/those	**quello/quelli**	kooaylloa/kooayllee
the one in the window/in the display case	**quello in vetrina/ sullo scaffale**	kooaylloa een vaytreenah/ soolloa skahffarlay
It's over there.	**È laggiù.**	ai lahdjoo

Defining the article

I'd like a... one.	**Ne vorrei un...**	nay vorraiee oon
big	**grande**	grahnday
cheap	**economico**	aykoanawmeekoa
dark	**scuro**	skooroa
good	**buono**	bwawnoa
heavy	**pesante**	payssahntay
large	**largo**	lahrgoa
light (weight)	**leggero**	laydjairoa
light (colour)	**chiaro**	keearroa
oval	**ovale**	ovarlay
rectangular	**rettangolare**	rehttahngolarray
round	**rotondo**	rotoandoa
small	**piccolo**	peekkoaloa
square	**quadrato**	kwahdrartoa
sturdy	**forte**	fortay
I don't want anything too expensive.	**Non voglio qualcosa di troppo caro.**	noan volyoa kwahlkawssah dee troppoa karroa

Preference

Can you show me some more?	**Me ne può mostrare degli altri?**	may nay pwo moastrarray daylyee ahltree
Haven't you anything...?	**Non ha qualcosa...?**	noan ah kwahlkawssah
cheaper/better	**meno caro/migliore**	maynoa karroa/meelyoaray
larger/smaller	**più largo/più piccolo**	peeoo lahrgoa/peeoo peekkoaloa

How much?

How much is this?	**Quanto costa questo?**	kwahntoa kostah kooaystoa
How much are they?	**Quanto costano?**	kwahntoa kostahnoa
I don't understand.	**Non capisco.**	noan kahpeeskoa
Please write it down.	**Per favore, me lo scriva.**	pair fahvoaray may loa skreevah
I don't want to spend more than 5.000 lire.	**Non voglio spendere più di 5.000 lire.**	noan volyoa spehndayray peeoo dee 5.000 leeray

FOR COLOURS, see page 113

Decision

That's just what I want.	È proprio quello che volevo.	ai prawpreeoa kooaylloa kay voalayvoa
It's not quite what I want.	Non è ciò che volevo.	noan ai cho kay voalayvoa
No, I don't like it.	No, non mi piace.	noa noan mee peearchay
I'll take it.	Lo prendo.	loa prayndoa

Ordering

| Can you order it for me? | Può ordinarmelo? | pwo oardeenahrmayloa |
| How long will it take? | Quanto tempo ci sarà da aspettare? | kwahntoa tehmpoa chee sahrah dah ahspehttarray |

Delivery

I'll take it with me.	Lo porto via.	loa portoa veeah
Deliver it to the... Hotel.	Lo consegni all'Albergo...	loa konsayñee ahllahlbayrgoa
Please send it to this address.	Per favore, lo mandi a questo indirizzo.	pair fahvoaray loa mahndee ah kooaystoa eendeereettsoa
Will I have any difficulty with the customs?	Avrò delle difficoltà alla dogana?	ahvroa dayllay deeffeekoaltah ahllah doagarnah

Paying

How much is it?	Quant'è?	kwahntai
Can I pay by traveller's cheque?	Accettate i traveller's cheque?	ahdchehttartay ee "traveller's cheque"
Do you accept dollars/pounds?	Accettate dei dollari/delle sterline?	ahtchehttartay daiee dollarree/dayllay stayrleenay
Do you accept credit cards?	Accettate carte di credito?	ahtchehttartay kahrtay dee kraydeetoa
Haven't you made a mistake in the bill?	Non vi siete sbagliati nel fare il conto?	noan vee seeaytay sbahlyeeartee nayl farray eel koantoa

Anything else?

No, thanks, that's all.	**No grazie, è tutto.**	noa **grart**seeay ai **toot**toa
Yes, I want...	**Sì, desidero...**	see day**zee**dayroa
Show me...	**Mi mostri...**	mee **moa**stree
Thank you. Good-bye.	**Grazie. Arrivederci.**	**grart**seeay ahrreevay-**dair**chee

Dissatisfied

Can you please exchange this?	**Può cambiare questo, per favore?**	pwo kahmbee**array** kooay**stoa** pair fah**voa**ray
I want to return this.	**Desidero rendere questo.**	day**zee**dayroa **raynd**ayray kooay**stoa**
I'd like a refund. Here's the receipt.	**Desidero essere rimborsato. Ecco la ricevuta.**	day**zee**dayroa **ehsss**ayray reemboar**sar**toa, **ehk**koa lah reechay**voo**tah

Posso aiutarla?	Can I help you?
Cosa desidera?	What would you like?
Che...desidera?	What...would you like?
colore/forma qualità/quantità	colour/shape quality/quantity
Mi dispiace, non ne abbiamo.	I'm sorry, we haven't any.
L'abbiamo esaurito.	We're out of stock.
Dobbiamo ordinarglielo?	Shall we order it for you?
Lo porta via o dobbiamo mandarglielo?	Will you take it with you or shall we send it?
Null'altro?	Anything else?
Sono...lire, per favore.	That's...lire, please.
La cassa è laggiù.	The cashier's over there.

SHOPPING GUIDE

Bookshop – Stationer's – News-stand

In Italy, bookshops and stationers' are usually separate shops, though the latter will often sell paperbacks. Newspapers and magazines are sold at news-stands.

Where's the nearest...?	Dov'è... più vicina ?	doavai... peeoo veecheenah
bookshop	la libreria	lah leebrayreeah
stationer's	la cartoleria	lah kahrtoalayreeah
news-stand	l'edicola	laydeekoalah
Where can I buy an English-language newspaper ?	Dove posso acquistare un giornale in inglese ?	doavay posssoa ahkkooeestarray oon joarnarlay een eengglayssay
I want to buy a/an/ some...	Desidero comprare...	dayzeedayroa koamprarray
address book	un'agenda per gli indirizzi	oonahjayndah pair lyee eendeereettsee
ball-point pen	una penna a sfera	oonah paynnah ah sfayrah
book	un libro	oon leebroa
box of paints	una scatola di colori	oonah skartoalah dee koaloree
carbon paper	della carta carbone	dayllah kahrtah kahrboanay
cellophane tape	del nastro adesivo	dayl nahstroa ahdayzeevoa
crayons	dei pastelli	daiee pahstehllee
dictionary Italian-English	un dizionario italiano-inglese	oon deetseeoanarreeoa eetahleearnoa / eengglayssay
drawing paper	della carta da disegno	dayllah kahrtah dah deessayñoa
drawing pins	delle puntine da disegno	dayllay poonteenay dah deessayñoa
envelopes	delle buste	dayllay boostay
eraser	una gomma	oonah goammah
file	una lima	oonah leemah
fountain pen	una penna stilografica	oonah paynnah steeloagrarfeekah
glue	della colla	dayllah kollah
guide-book	una guida	oonah gooeedah
ink black/red/blue	dell'inchiostro nero/rosso/blu	daylleengkeeostroa nayroa/roasssoa/bloo
labels	delle etichette	dayllay ayteekehttay
magazine	una rivista	oonah reeveestah

map	una carta geografica	oonah kahrtah jayoagrarfeekah
map of the town	una pianta della città	oonah peeahntah dayllah cheettah
road map of...	una carta stradale di...	oonah kahrtah strahdarlay dee
newspaper	un giornale	oon joarnarlay
notebook	un taccuino	oon tahkkooeenoa
note paper	della carta da lettere	dayllah kahrtah dah lehttayray
paperback	un libro tascabile	oon leebroa tahskarbeelay
paper napkins	dei tovaglioli di carta	daiee toavahlyoalee dee kahrtah
paste	della colla forte	dayllah kollah fortay
pen	una penna	oonah paynnah
pencil	una matita	oonah mahteetah
pencil sharpener	un temperino	oon taympayreenoa
playing cards	delle carte da gioco	dayllay kahrtay dah jokoa
postcards	delle cartoline	dayllay kahrtoaleenay
refill (for a pen)	un ricambio (per una penna)	oon reekambeeoa (pair oonah paynnah)
rubber	una gomma	oonah goammah
ruler	una riga	oonah reegah
string	dello spago	daylloa spargoa
tissue paper	della carta velina	dayllah kahrtah vayleenah
typewriter ribbon	un nastro per macchina da scrivere	oon nahstroa pair mahkkeenah dah skreevayray
typing paper	della carta per macchina da scrivere	dayllah kahrtah pair mahkkeenah dah skreevayray
wrapping paper	della carta da pacchi	dayllah kahrtah dah pahkkee
writing pad	un blocco per appunti	oon blokkoa pair appoontee
Where's the guidebook section?	Dov'è il reparto delle guide?	doavai eel raypahrtoa dayllay gooeeday
Where do you keep the English books?	Dov'è il reparto dei libri inglesi?	doavai eel raypahrtoa daiee leebree eengglayssee

Here are some contemporary Italian authors whose books are available in English translation:

Dino Buzzati	Primo Levi
Carlo Cassola	Curzio Malaparte
Natalia Ginzburg	Alberto Moravia
Giovanni Guareschi	Ignazio Silone

Camping

Here we're concerned with the equipment you may need.

I'd like a/an/some...	Vorrei...	vorraiee
axe	una scure	oonah skooray
bottle-opener	un apribottiglia	oon ahpreebotteelyah
bucket	un secchio	oon saykkeeoa
butane gas	del gas butano	dayl gaz bootarnoa
camp bed	un letto da campo	oon lehttoa dah kahmpoa
camping equipment	un equipaggiamento da campeggio	oon aykooeepahdjahmayntoa dah kahmpaydjoa
can opener	un apriscatole	oon ahpreeskahtoalay
(folding) chair	una sedia (pieghevole)	oonah saydeeah (peeaygayvoalay)
compass	una bussola	oonah boosssoalah
corkscrew	un cavatappi	oon kahvahtahppee
crockery	delle stoviglie	dayllay stoaveelyay
cutlery	delle posate	dayllay poassartay
deck-chair	una sedia a sdraio	oonah saydeeah ah sdrareeoa
first-aid kit	una cassetta del pronto soccorso	oonah kahsssehttah dayl proantoa soakkoarsoa
flashlight	una lampadina tascabile	oonah lahmpahdeenah tahskarbeelay
frying-pan	una padella	oonah pahdehllah
groundsheet	un telo per il terreno	oon tayloa pair eel tayrraynoa
hammer	un martello	oon mahrtehlloa
hammock	un'amaca	oonarmahkah
kerosene	del kerosene	dayl kayroassaynay
knapsack	uno zaino	oonoa dzaheenoa
lamp	una lampada	oonah lahmpahdah
lantern	una lanterna	oonah lahntehrnah
matches	dei fiammiferi	daiee feeahmmeefayree
mattress	un materasso	oon mahtayrahsssoa
methylated spirits	dell'alcool metilico	dayllahlkoal mayteeleekoa
mosquito net	una zanzariera	oonah zahnzarreeayrah
pail	un secchio	oon saykkeeoa
paraffin	del kerosene	dayl kayroassaynay
picnic case	un cestino da pic-nic	oon chaysteenoa dah "pic-nic"
pressure cooker	una pentola a pressione	oonah payntoalah ah prayssseeoanay
primus stove	un fornello a petrolio	oon foarnehlloa ah paytroaleeoa

rope	della fune	dayllah foonay
rucksack	un sacco da montagna	oon sahkkoa dah moantarñah
saucepan	una casseruola	oonah kahsssayroooalah
scissors	un paio di forbici	oon pareeoa dee foarbeechee
screwdriver	un cacciavite	oon kahtchahveetay
sleeping bag	un sacco a pelo	oon sahkkoa ah payloa
stewpan	una pentola	oonah payntoalah
stove	una stufa	oonah stoofah
(folding) table	una tavola (pieghevole)	oonah tarvoalah (peeaygayvoalay)
tent	una tenda	oonah tayndah
tent-peg	un picchetto per tenda	oon peekkehttoa pair tayndah
tent-pole	un palo per tenda	oon parloa pair tayndah
thermos flask (bottle)	un termos	oon tehrmoass
tin-opener	un apriscatole	oon ahpreeskartoalay
tongs	un paio di tenaglie	oon pareeoa dee taynarlyay
tool kit	una cassetta attrezzi	oonah kahsssehttah ahttrehttsee
water carrier	un bidone per l'acqua	oon beedoanay pair lahkkwah
wood alcohol	dell'alcool metilico	dayllahlkoal mayteeleekoa

Crockery

beakers (tumblers)	i bicchieri	ee beekkeeairee
cups	le tazze	lay tahttsay
food box	la cassetta per il cibo	lah kahsssehttah pair eel cheeboa
mugs	i boccali	ee boakkarlee
plates	i piatti	ee peeahttee
saucers	i piattini	ee peeahtteenee

Cutlery

forks	le forchette	lay forkehttay
knives	i coltelli	ee koaltehllee
spoons	i cucchiai	ee kookkeeighee
teaspoons	i cucchiaini	ee kookkeeigheenee
(made of) plastic	(in) plastica	(een) plarsteekah
(made of) stainless steel	(in) acciaio inossidabile	(een) ahtchigheeoa eenoasssseedarbeelay

Chemist's – Drugstore

The Italian chemists' normally don't stock the great range of goods that you'll find in England or the U.S. For example, they don't sell photographic equipment or books. And for perfume, make-up, etc., you must go to a *profumeria* (proafoomay**ree**ah).

You can recognize a chemist's by the sign outside—a green or red cross, illuminated at night. In the window you'll see a notice telling where the nearest all-night chemist's is.

This section is divided into two parts:

1. Pharmaceutical – medicine, first-aid, etc.
2. Toiletry – toilet articles, cosmetics.

General

Where's the nearest (all-night) chemist's?	**Dov'è la farmacia (di turno) più vicina?**	doavai lah fahrmah**chee**ah (dee **toor**noa) peeoo vee**chee**nah
What time does the chemist's open/close?	**A che ora apre/chiude la farmacia?**	ah kay oarah arpray/keeooday lah fahrmah-**chee**ah

Part 1 – Pharmaceutical

I want something for...	**Desidero qualcosa per...**	dayzeedayroa kwahl**kaws**sah pair
a cold	**il raffreddore**	eel rahffrayd**doa**ray
a cough	**la tosse**	lah **toass**say
hay fever	**la febbre del fieno**	lah **fayb**bray dayl feeaynoa
a hangover	**un mal di capo**	oon mahl dee **kar**poa
sunburn	**una scottatura solare**	oonah skoattar**too**rah soalarray
travel sickness	**il mal d'auto**	eel mahl **dow**toa
an upset stomach	**il mal di stomaco**	eel mahl dee **stoa**mahkoa
Can you make up this prescription for me?	**Può prepararmi questa ricetta?**	pwo praypah**rarr**mee kooaystah reechehttah
Shall I wait?	**Devo aspettare?**	**day**voa ahspeht**tarr**ay

FOR DOCTOR, see page 162

When shall I come back ?	Quando devo ritornare ?	kwahndoa dayvoa reetoarnarray
Can I get it without a prescription ?	Può darmi questa medicina senza ricetta ?	pwo darrmee kooaystah maydeecheenah sayntsah reechehttah
Can I have a/an/ some...?	Mi può dare...?	mee pwo darray
antiseptic cream	della crema anti-settica	dayllah kraimah ahntee-ssehtteekah
aspirin	delle aspirine	dayllay ahspeereenay
bandage crepe/gauze	delle bende crespate/di garza	dayllay baynday krayspartay/dee gahrdzah
Band-Aids	dei cerotti	daiee chayrottee
castor oil	dell'olio di ricino	daylloleeoa dee reecheenoa
contraceptives	degli antifecon-dativi	daylyee ahnteefaykoandah-teevee
corn plasters	un callifugo	oon kahlleefoogoa
cotton wool	del cotone idrofilo	dayl koatoanay eedroa-feeloa
cough drops	delle gocce per la tosse	dayllay goatchay pair lah toasssay
disinfectant	del disinfettante	dayl deesseenfehttahntay
ear drops	delle gocce per le orecchie	dayllay goatchay pair lay awraykkeeay
Elastoplast	dei cerotti	daiee chayrottee
eye drops	delle gocce per gli occhi	dayllay goatchay pair lyee okkee
gargle	un liquido per gargarismi	oon leekooeedoa pair gahrgahreesmee
insect repellent	una crema insetti-cida	oonah kraimah eensehttee-cheedah
iodine	della tintura di iodio	dayllah teentoorah dee eeodeeoa
laxative	un lassativo	oon lahsssahteevoa
mouthwash	un disinfettante per la bocca	oon deesseenfehttahntay pair lah boakkah
sanitary napkins	degli assorbenti igienici	daylyee ahsssoarbayntee eejayneechee
sedative	un sedativo	oon saydahteevoa
sleeping pills	dei sonniferi	daiee soanneefayree
stomach pills	delle pillole per lo stomaco	dayllay peelloalay pair loa stomahkoa
throat lozenges	delle pasticche per la gola	dayllay pahsteekkay pair lah goalah

Part 2 – Toiletry

I'd like a/an/some...	Desidero...	dayzeedayroa
acne-cream	una crema per l'acne	oonah kraimah pair lahknay
after-shave lotion	una lozione dopobarba	oonah loatseeoanay dawpoabahrbah
astringent	un astringente	oonahstreenjayntay
bath essence	un profumo da bagno	oon proafoomoa dah barñoa
cologne	dell'acqua di colonia	dayllahkkwah dee koaloneeah
cream	una crema	oonah kraimah
cleansing cream	una crema detergente	oonah kraimah daytehrjayntay
cuticle cream	una crema per le pellicine	oonah kraimah pair lay paylleecheenay
foundation cream	una crema di base	oonah kraimah dee barzay
moisturizing cream	una crema idratante	oonah kraimah eedrahtahntay
night cream	una crema da notte	oonah kraimah dah nottay
deodorant	un deodorante	oon dayoadoarahntay
emery board	una limetta per unghie	oonah leemehttah pair oonggeeay
eye liner	un eye-liner	oon "eye-liner"
eye pencil	una matita per occhi	oonah mahteetah pair okkee
face pack	una maschera di bellezza	oonah mahskayrah dee behllehttsah
face powder	della cipria	dayllah cheepreeah
foot cream	una crema per i piedi	oonah kraimah pair ee peeaydee
hand cream	una crema per le mani	oonah kraimah pair lay marnee
lipsalve	un burro cacao	oon boorroa kahkaroa
lipstick	un rossetto	oon roasssehttoa
lipstick brush	un pennello per il rossetto	oon paynnehlloa pair eel roasssehttoa
make-up remover pads	dei tamponi per togliere il trucco	daiee tahmpoanee pair tolyeeray eel trookkoa
nail clippers	un tagliaunghie	oon tahlyahoonggeeay
nail file	una lima da unghie	oonah leemah dah oonggeeay
nail polish	uno smalto per unghie	oonoa smahltoa pair oonggeeay

nail polish remover	dell'acetone	dayllahchaytoanay
nail scissors	un paio di forbicine per le unghie	oon pareeoa dee forbee-cheenay pair lay oonggeeay
perfume	un profumo	oon proafoomoa
powder	della cipria	dayllah cheepreeah
razor	un rasoio	oon rahssoaeeoa
rouge	un belletto	oon behllehttoa
safety pins	delle spille di sicurezza	dayllay speellay dee seekoorayttsah
shampoo	uno shampoo	oonoa "shampoo"
shaving brush	un pennello da barba	oon paynnehlloa dah bahrbah
shaving cream	una crema da barba	oonah kraimah dah bahrbah
soap	del sapone	dayl sahpoanay
sun-tan cream	una crema solare	oonah kraimah soalarray
sun-tan oil	un olio solare	oonawleeoa soalarray
talcum powder	del talco	dayl tahlkoa
tissues	dei fazzolettini di carta	daiee fahddzoalehtteenee dee kahrtah
toilet paper	della carta igienica	dayllah kahrtah eejay-neekah
toilet water	dell'acqua da toletta	dayllahkkwah dah toa-lehttah
toothbrush	uno spazzolino da denti	oonoa spahttsoaleenoa dah dehntee
toothpaste	un dentifricio	oon daynteefreechoa
tweezers	delle pinzette	dayllay peentsehttay

For your hair

bobby pins	delle forcine	dayllay foarcheenay
brush	una spazzola per capelli	oonah spahttsoalah pair kahpayllee
comb	un pettine	oon paytteenay
curlers	dei bigodini	daiee beegoadeenee
dye	una tintura	oonah teentoorah
grips	delle forcelle	dayllay foarchayllay
lacquer	della lacca	dayllah lahkkah
oil	della brillantina	dayllah breellahnteenah
pins	delle mollette	dayllay moallayttay
rollers	dei rullini	daiee roolleenee
setting lotion	una lozione fissativa	oonah loatseeoanay feesssahteevah
tint	una sfumatura	oonah sfoomahtoorah

Clothing

If you want to buy something specific, prepare yourself in advance. Look at the list of clothing on page 117. Get some idea of the colour, material and size you want.
They're all listed on the next few pages.

General

I'd like...	**Vorrei...**	vorraiee
I want...for a 10-year-old boy.	**Desidero...per un bambino di 10 anni.**	dayzeedayroa... pair oon bahmbeenoa dee 10 ahnnee
I want something like this.	**Voglio qualcosa come questo.**	volyoa kwahlkawssah koamay kooaystoa
I like the one in the window.	**Mi piace quello in vetrina.**	mee peearchay kooaylloa een vaytreenah
How much is that per metre?	**Quanto costa al metro?**	kwahntoa kostah ahl maytroa

1 centimetre = 0.39 in.	1 inch = 2.54 cm.
1 metre = 39.37 in.	1 foot = 30.5 cm.
10 metres = 32.81 ft.	1 yard = 0.91 m.

Colour

I want something in...	**Voglio qualcosa di colore...**	volyoa kwahlkawssah dee koaloaray
I want a darker shade.	**Desidero una tonalità più scura.**	dayzeedayroa oonah toanahleetah peeoo skoorah
I want something to match this.	**Voglio qualcosa per ravvivare questo.**	volyoa kwahlkawssah pair rahvveevarray kooaystoa
I don't like the colour.	**Non mi piace il colore.**	noan mee peearchay eel koaloaray

righe	**pallini**	**quadri**	**fantasia**
(reegay)	(pahlleenee)	(kwardree)	(fahntahzeeah)

beige	**beige**	baij
black	**nero**	**nay**roa
blue	**blu**	bloo
brown	**marrone**	mahr**ro**anay
cream	**crema**	**krai**mah
crimson	**cremisi**	krai**mee**zee
emerald	**smeraldo**	smay**rah**ldoa
fawn	**fulvo**	**fool**voa
gold	**oro**	**o**roa
green	**verde**	**vayr**day
grey	**grigio**	**gree**joa
mauve	**malva**	**mahl**vah
orange	**arancio**	ar**rahn**choa
pink	**rosa**	**raw**zah
purple	**porporino**	poarpoa**ree**noa
red	**rosso**	**roass**soa
scarlet	**scarlatto**	skahr**laht**toa
silver	**argento**	ahr**jayn**toa
turquoise	**turchese**	toor**kay**zay
white	**bianco**	bee**ahng**koa
yellow	**giallo**	**jahl**loa

Material

Do you have anything in...?	**Ha qualcosa in...?**	ah kwahl**kaw**ssah een
I want a cotton blouse.	**Voglio una blusa di cotone.**	**vol**yoa **oo**nah **bloo**ssah dee koa**toa**nay
Is that...?	**È un prodotto...?**	ai oon proa**doat**toa
hand-made	**fatto a mano**	**faht**toa ah **mar**noa
imported	**importato**	eempoar**tar**toa
made here	**nazionale**	nahtsee**oa**narlay
I want something thinner.	**Desidero qualcosa di più fine.**	dayzee**day**roa kwahl**kaw**ssah dee pee**oo fee**nay
Do you have any better quality?	**Ha una qualità migliore?**	ah **oo**nah kwahlee**tah** meel**yoar**ay
What's it made of?	**Di che cosa è fatto?**	dee kay **kaw**ssah ai **faht**toa

It may be made of...

cambric	il percalle	eel payrkahllay
camel-hair	il pelo di cammello	eel payloa dee kahm-mehlloa
chiffon	lo chiffon	loa sheeffoan
corduroy	il velluto a coste	eel vayllootoa ah koastay
cotton	il cotone	eel koatoanay
crepe	il crespo	eel krayspoa
felt	il feltro	eel fayltroa
flannel	la flannella	lah flahnnehllah
gabardine	il gabardine	eel gahbahrdeen
lace	il pizzo	eel peettsoa
leather	la pelle	lah pehllay
linen	il lino	eel leenoa
piqué	il picchè	eel peekkai
poplin	il popeline	eel poapayleen
rayon	il rayon	eel rareeoan
satin	il raso	eel rarssoa
serge	la saia	lah sareeah
silk	la seta	lah saytah
suede	la renna	lah rehnnah
terrycloth	il tessuto di spugna	eel taysssootoa dee spooñah
tulle	il tulle	eel toollay
tweed	il tweed	eel "tweed"
velvet	il velluto	eel vayllootoa
velveteen	il velluto di cotone	eel vayllootoa dee koatoanay
wool	la lana	lah larnah
worsted	il pettinato	eel paytteenartoa
synthetic	sintetico	seentayteekoa
wash and wear	non si stira	noan see steerah
wrinkle resistant	ingualcibile	eengwahlcheebeelay

Size

My size is 38.	La mia misura è il 38.	lah meeah meezoorah ai eel 38
Could you measure me?	Può prendermi le misure?	pwo prehndayrmee lay meezooray
I don't know the Italian sizes.	Non conosco le misure italiane.	noan koanoaskoa lay meezooray eetahleearnay

In that case, look at the charts on the next page.

This is your size

In Europe sizes vary somewhat from country to country, so this table must be taken as an approximate guide.

Ladies

Dresses/Suits						
American	10	12	14	16	18	20
British	32	34	36	38	40	42
Continental	38	40	42	44	46	48

Stockings							Shoes			
American } British }	8	8½	9	9½	10	10½	6 4½	7 5½	8 6½	9 7½
Continental	0	1	2	3	4	5	37	38	40	41

Gentlemen

Suits/Overcoats							Shirts			
American } British }	36	38	40	42	44	46	15	16	17	18
Continental	46	48	50	52	54	56	38	41	43	45

Shoes									
American } British }	5	6	7	8	8½	9	9½	10	11
Continental	38	39	41	42	43	43	44	44	45

A good fit?

Can I try it on?	**Posso provarlo?**	**poss**soa provahrloa
Where's the fitting room?	**Dov'è la cabina di prova?**	doavai lah kah**bee**nah dee **prawv**vah
Is there a mirror?	**C'è uno specchio?**	chai oonoa **spaykk**eeoa
Does it fit?	**Va bene?**	vah **bai**nay
It fits very well.	**Va molto bene.**	vah **moal**toa **bai**nay

FOR NUMBERS, see page 175

SHOPPING GUIDE

It doesn't fit.	**Non va bene.**	noan vah **bai**nay
It's too...	**È troppo...**	ai **trop**poa
short/long	**corto/lungo**	**koar**toa/**loong**goa
tight/loose	**stretto/largo**	**strayt**toa/**lahr**goa
How long will it take to alter?	**Quanto tempo ci vuole per le modifiche?**	**kwahn**toa **tehm**poa chee **vwo**lay pair lay moa**dee**feekay

Shoes

I'd like a pair of...	**Vorrei un paio di...**	vor**raiee** oon **par**eeoa dee
shoes/sandals	**scarpe/sandali**	**skahr**pay/**sahn**dahlee
boots/slippers	**stivali/pantofole**	**stee**varlee/**pahn**tofoalay
These are too...	**Queste sono troppo...**	**kooay**stay **soa**noa **trop**poa
narrow/wide	**strette/larghe**	**strayt**tay/**lahr**gay
large/small	**grandi/piccole**	**grahn**dee/**peek**koalay
They pinch my toes.	**Mi fanno male alle punte dei piedi.**	mee **fahn**noa **mar**lay **ahl**lay **poon**tay **dai**ee **pee**aydee
Do you have a larger size?	**Ha uno numero più grande?**	ah **oo**noa **noo**mayroa **peeoo grahn**day
I want a smaller size.	**Desidero uno numero più piccolo.**	day**zee**dayroa **oo**noa **noo**mayroa **peeoo peek**koaloa
Do you have the same in...?	**Ha lo stesso in...?**	ah loa **stayss**soa een
brown/beige	**marrone/beige**	mahr**roa**nay/baij
black/white	**nero/bianco**	**nay**roa/**bee**ahngkoa
I'd like a shoe polish.	**Vorrei del lucido.**	vor**raiee** dayl **loo**cheedoa

Shoes worn out? Here's the key to getting them fixed again:

Can you repair these shoes?	**Mi può riparare queste scarpe?**	mee pwo reepah**rar**ray **kooay**stay **skahr**pay
Can you stitch this?	**Può attaccare questo?**	pwo ahttahk**kar**ray **kooay**stoa
I want new soles and heels.	**Desidero suole e tacchi nuovi.**	day**zee**dayroa **swo**lay ay **tahk**kee **nwaw**vee
When will they be ready?	**Quando saranno pronte?**	**kwahn**doa sah**rahn**noa **proan**tay

Clothes and accessories

I'd like a/an/some...	Vorrei...	vorraiee
anorak	una giacca a vento	oonah jahkkah ah vayntoa
bath robe	un accappatoio	oon ahkkahppahtoaeeoa
bathing cap	una cuffia da bagno	oonah kooffeeah dah barñoa
bathing suit	un costume da bagno	oon koastoomay dah barñoa
blouse	una blusa	oonah bloozah
boots	degli stivali	daylyee steevarlee
bow tie	una cravatta a farfalla	oonah krahvahttah ah fahrfahllah
bra	un reggiseno	oon raydjeessehnoa
braces	delle bretelle	dayllay braytehllay
briefs	delle mutande da uomo	dayllay mootahnday dah ooomoa
cap	un berretto	oon bayrrayttoa
cardigan	una giacca di lana	oonah jahkkah dee larnah
coat	un soprabito	oon soaprarbeetoa
dinner jacket	uno smoking	oonoa "smoking"
dress	un vestito	oon vaysteetoa
dressing gown	una veste da camera	oonah vehstay dah karmayrah
evening dress (woman's)	un abito da sera	oon arbeetoa dah sayrah
frock	un abito	oon arbeetoa
girdle	un busto	oon boostoa
gloves	dei guanti	daiee gwahntee
handkerchief	un fazzoletto	oon fahddzoalehttoa
hat	un cappello	oon kahppehlloa
jacket	una casacca	oonah kahssahkkah
jeans	dei jeans	daiee "jeans"
jersey	una camicetta a maglia	oonah kahmeecehttah ah marlyah
jumper (Br.)	un maglione	oon mahlyoanay
negligé	un negligé	oon naygleejay
nightdress	una camicia da notte	oonah kahmeechah dah nottay
overalls	una tuta	oonah tootah
panties	dei calzoncini da donna	daiee kahltsoancheenee dah donnah
panty-girdle	un corsetto	oon koarsayttoa
panty hose	dei collant	daiee koallahnt
parka	una giacca a vento	oonah jahkkah ah vayntoa
pinafore	un grembiulino	oon graymbeeooleenoa

pyjamas	un pigiama	oon peejarmah
raincoat	un impermeabile	oon eempayrmayarbeelay
robe	un mantello	oon mahntehlloa
sandals	dei sandali	daiee sahndahlee
scarf	una sciarpa	oonah shahrpah
shirt	una camicia	oonah kahmeechah
shoes	delle scarpe	dayllay skahrpay
skirt	una gonna	oonah goannah
slip	una sottoveste	oonah soattoavehstay
slippers	delle pantofole	dayllay pahntofoalay
socks	dei calzini	daiee kahltseenee
sports jacket	una giacca sportiva	oonah jahkkah sporteevah
stockings	delle calze da donna	dayllay kahltsay dah donnah
suit (man's)	un completo	oon koamplaytoa
suit (woman's)	un abito	oon arbeetoa
suspenders	delle bretelle	dayllay braytehllay
sweater	una giacchetta	oonah jahkkayttah
sweatshirt	una giacca da ginnastica	oonah jahkkah dah jeennarsteekah
T-shirt	una canottiera	oonah kahnoatteeayrah
tennis shoes	delle scarpe da tennis	dayllay skahrpay dah "tennis"
tie	una cravatta	oonah krahvahttah
tights	una calzamaglia	oonah kahlsahmarlyah
top coat	un cappotto	oon kahppoattoa
track suit	un completo per atletica	oon koamplaytoa pair ahtlayteekah
trousers	dei pantaloni	daiee pahntahloanee
underpants (men)	delle mutande da uomo	dayllay mootahnday dah ooomoa
undershirt	una camiciola	oonah kahmeecholah
vest (Am.)	un panciotto	oon pahnchottoa
vest (Br.)	una camiciola	oonah kahmeecholah
waistcoat	un panciotto	oon pahnchottoa

belt	la cintura	lah cheentoorah
buckle	la fibbia	lah feebbeeah
button	il bottone	eel boattoanay
cuffs	i polsini	ee poalseenee
elastic	l'elastico	laylahsteekoa
pocket	la tasca	lah tarskah
shoe laces	i lacci delle scarpe	ee latchee dayllay skahrpay
zip (zipper)	la cerniera	lah chehrneeayrah

Electrical appliances and accessories – Records

In most large cities in Italy you'll find voltage for electric lights at 110–127 AC, 50–cycle and voltage for appliances at 220 or 230 AC, 50–cycle. This is part of a national plan calling for two different circuits, each with its own meters. In Italian-speaking Switzerland, you'll likely find 220–volt, 50–cycle current. Check the voltage before you plug your appliance in. You'll find an adaptor useful since the round pins on continental plugs are different from ours.

What's the voltage?	**Qual'è il voltaggio?**	kwarlai eel voaltahdjoa
I want a plug for this...	**Desidero una spina per questo...**	dayzeedayroa oonah speenah pair kooaystoa
Do you have a battery for this?	**Ha una batteria per questo?**	ah oonah bahttayreeah pair kooaystoa
This is broken. Can you repair it?	**È rotto. Me lo può riparare?**	ai roattoa. may loa pwo reepahrarray
When will it be ready?	**Quando sarà pronto?**	kwahndoa sahrah proantoa
I'd like a/an/some...	**Vorrei...**	vorraiee
adaptor	**una presa multipla**	oonah prayzah mooltee-plah
amplifier	**un amplificatore**	oon ahmpleefeekahtoaray
battery	**una batteria**	oonah bahttayreeah
blender	**un frullatore**	oon froollahtoaray
(wall) clock	**un orologio (da muro)**	oon oaroalojoa (dah mooroa)
food mixer	**un frullino**	oon froolleenoa
hair dryer	**un asciugacapelli**	oon ashoogahkahpayllee
(travelling) iron	**un ferro da stiro (da viaggio)**	oon fehrroa dah steeroa (dah veeahdjoa)
kettle	**un bollitore**	oon boalleetoaray
percolator	**una macchinetta per il caffè**	oonah mahkkeenehttah pair eel kahffai
plug	**una spina**	oonah speenah
portable...	**...portatile**	...poartarteelay
radio	**una radio**	oonah rardeeoa
car radio	**un'autoradio**	unowtoarardeeoa
record player	**un giradischi**	oon jeerahdeeskee
shaver	**un rasoio**	oon rahssoaeeoa
speakers	**degli altoparlanti**	daylyee ahltoapahrlahntee

tape recorder	**un registratore**	oon rayjeestrahtoaray
cassette tape recorder	**un registratore a cassette**	oon rayjeestrahtoaray ah kasssayttay
television	**un televisore**	oon taylayveezoaray
colour television	**un televisore a colori**	oon taylayveezoaray ah koaloaree
toaster	**un tostapane**	oon toastahparnay
transformer	**un trasformatore**	oon trahsfoarmahtoaray

Record shop

Do you have any records by...?	**Avete dischi di...?**	ahvaytay deeskee dee
Can I listen to this record?	**Posso ascoltare questo disco?**	posssoa ahskoaltarray kooaystoa deeskoa
I'd like a cassette.	**Vorrei una cassetta.**	vorraiee oonah kahsssayttah
I want a new needle.	**Vorrei una puntina nuova.**	vorraiee oonah poonteenah nwawvah

L.P. (33 rpm)	**33 giri**	trayntahtrai jeeree
E.P. (45 rpm)	**super 45 giri**	soopair kwahrahntahcheengkooay jeeree
single	**45 giri**	kwahrahntahcheengkooay jeeree

chamber music	**musica da camera**	moozeekah dah karmayrah
classical music	**musica classica**	moozeekah klahssseekah
folk music	**musica folcloristica**	moozeekah folkloreesteekah
instrumental music	**musica strumentale**	moozeekah stroomayntarlay
jazz	**jazz**	jazz
light music	**musica leggera**	moozeekah laydjairah
orchestral music	**musica d'orchestra**	moozeekah doarkehstrah
pop music	**musica pop**	moozeekah pop

Here are the names of a few popular recording artists:

Adriano Celentano	Domenico Modugno
Gigliola Cinquetti	Gianni Morandi
Sergio Endrigo	Rita Pavone
Milva	Patty Pravo
Mina	Massimo Ranieri

Hairdressing – Barber's

I don't speak much Italian.	**Non parlo molto l'italiano.**	noan **pahrloa moaltoa** leetahleearnoa
I'm in a hurry.	**Ho fretta.**	oa **frayttah**
I want a haircut, please.	**Per favore, mi tagli i capelli.**	pair fahvoaray mee **tarlyee** ee kah**payllee**
I'd like a shave.	**Vorrei che mi radesse.**	vorraiee kay mee rah**daysssay**
Don't cut it too short.	**Non li tagli troppo corti.**	noan lee **tarlyee troppoa koartee**
Scissors only, please.	**Solo con le forbici, per favore.**	**soaloa** kon lay **foarbee**-chee pair fahvoaray
A razor cut, please.	**Col rasoio, per favore.**	kol rah**ssoaeeoa** pair fah**voaray**
Don't use the clippers.	**Non usi la macchinetta.**	noan **oozee** lah mahkkee**nehttah**
Just a trim, please.	**Solo una spuntatina, per favore.**	**soaloa oonah** spoontah**teenah** pair fahvoaray
That's enough off.	**Basta così.**	**bahstah kawssee**
A little more off the...	**Ancora un po'...**	ahng**koarah** oon po
back	**dietro**	dee**aytroa**
neck	**sul collo**	sool **kolloa**
sides	**ai lati**	ahee **lartee**
top	**in cima**	een **chee**mah
I don't want any cream.	**Non voglio della crema.**	noan **volyoa dayllah kraimah**
Would you please trim my...?	**Per favore, vuole spuntarmi...?**	pair **fahvoaray** vwawly spoon**tahrmee**
beard	**la barba**	lah **bahrbah**
moustache	**i baffi**	ee **bahffee**
sideboards (sideburns)	**le basette**	lay bah**zayttay**
Thank you. That's fine.	**Grazie. Va bene.**	**grartseeay.** vah **bainay**
How much do I owe you?	**Quanto le devo?**	**kwahntoa** lay **dayvoa**
This is for you.	**Questo è per lei.**	**kooaystoa** ai pair **laiee**

FOR TIPPING, see inside back-cover

Ladies' hairdressing

Is there a beauty salon in the hotel ?	C'è l'istituto di bellezza nell' albergo ?	chai leesteetootoa dee behllehttsah nayll-ahlbayrgoa
Can I make an appointment for some-time on Thursday ?	Posso avere un appuntamento per giovedì ?	posssoa ahvayray oon ahppoontahmayntoa pair joavaydee
I'd like it cut and shaped.	Vorrei il taglio e la messa in piega.	vorraiee eel tarlyoa ay lah maysssah een peeaygah
with a fringe (bangs)	con la frangia	kon lah frahnjah
page-boy style	alla paggio	ahllah pahdjoa
a razor cut	tagliati col rasoio	tahlyartee kol rahssoaeeoa
a re-style	una pettinatura diversa	oonah paytteenahtoorah deevayrsah
with ringlets	a riccioli	ah reetchoalee
with waves	ondulati	oandoolartee
in a bun	a crocchia	ah krokkeeah
I want a...	Voglio...	volyoa
bleach	la decolorazione	lah daykoaloarahtseeoanay
colour rinse	un cachet	oon kahshay
dye	la tintura	lah teentoorah
permanent	la permanente	lah pairmahnayntay
shampoo and set	shampoo e messa in piega	"shampoo" ay maysssah een peeaygah
tint	una sfumatura	oonah sfoomahtoorah
touch up	una ritoccatina	oonah reetoakkahteenah
the same colour	lo stesso colore	loa staysssoa koaloaray
a darker/a lighter colour	un colore più scuro/ più chiaro	oon koaloaray peeoo skooroa/peeoo keearroa
auburn/blond/ brunette	castano/biondo/ bruno	kahstarnoa/beeoandoa/ broonoa
Do you have a colour chart ?	Avete una tabella dei colori ?	ahvaytay oonah tahbayllah daiee koaloaree
I don't want any hairspray.	Non voglio lacca.	noan volyoa lahkkah
I want a...	Desidero...	dayzeedayroa
manicure	la manicure	lah mahneekoor
pedicure	la pedicure	lah paydeekoor
face-pack	il massaggio al viso	eel mahsssahdjoa ahl veezoa

Jeweller's – Watchmaker's

Can you repair this watch?	**Mi può riparare questo orologio?**	mee pwo reepahrarray kooaystoa oaroalojoa
The… is broken.	**…è rotto (rotta).**	ai **roatt**oa (**roatt**ah)
glass/spring	**il vetro/la molla**	eel **vaytr**oa/lah **moll**ah
strap	**il cinturino**	eel cheentoo**reen**oa
winder	**la chiavetta**	lah keeah**veht**tah
I want this watch cleaned.	**Voglio far pulire questo orologio.**	**vol**yoa fahr poo**leer**ay kooaystoa oaroalojoa
When will it be ready?	**Quando sarà pronto?**	**kwahnd**oa sah**rah proant**oa
Could I please see that?	**Mi fa vedere quello, per favore?**	mee fah vay**dayr**ay kooay**lloa** pair fah**voar**ay
I'm just looking around.	**Do solo un'occhiata.**	daw **soal**oa oonoakkee-**artah**
I want a small present for…	**Desidero un regalino per…**	day**zeed**ayroa oon raygah**leen**oa pair
I don't want anything too expensive.	**Non voglio qualcosa di troppo caro.**	noan **vol**yoa kwahl**kawss**ah dee **tropp**oa **karr**oa
I want something…	**Voglio qualcosa…**	**vol**yoa kwahl**kawss**ah
better	**migliore**	meel**yoar**ay
cheaper	**più economico**	pee**oo** aykoanaw**meek**oa
simpler	**più semplice**	pee**oo** saym**pleech**ay
Do you have anything in gold?	**Avete qualcosa in oro?**	ah**vayt**ay kwahl**kawss**ah een **oro**a
Is this real silver?	**È argento puro?**	ai ahr**jaynt**oa **poor**oa

If it's made of gold, ask:

How many carats is it?	**Quanti carati?**	**kwahnt**ee kah**rart**ee

When you go to a jeweller's, you've probably got some idea of what you want beforehand. Find out what the article is made of and then look up the name of the article itself in the following lists.

What's it made of?

amber	l'ambra	lahmbrah
amethyst	l'ametista	lahmayteestah
chromium	il cromo	eel kromoa
copper	il rame	eel rarmay
coral	il corallo	eel koarahlloa
crystal	il cristallo	eel kreestahlloa
cut glass	il vetro tagliato	eel vaytroa tahlyartoa
diamond	il diamante	eel deeahmahntay
ebony	l'ebano	laybahnoa
emerald	lo smeraldo	loa smayrahldoa
enamel	lo smalto	loa smahltoa
glass	il vetro	eel vaytroa
gold	l'oro	loroa
gold plate	la lamina d'oro	lah lahmeenah doroa
ivory	l'avorio	lahvoreeoa
jade	la giada	lah jardah
onyx	l'onice	loneechay
pearl	la perla	lah pehrlah
pewter	il peltro	eel payltroa
platinum	il platino	eel plarteenoa
ruby	il rubino	eel roobeenoa
sapphire	lo zaffiro	loa dzahffeeroa
silver	l'argento	lahrjayntoa
silver plate	l'argentatura	lahrjayntahtoorah
stainless steel	l'acciaio inossida-bile	lahtchareeoa eenoass-seedahbeelay
topaz	il topazio	eel toapartseeoa
turquoise	il turchese	eel toorkayzay

What is it?

I'd like a/an/some...	Vorrei...	vorraiee
bangle	un braccialetto rigido	oon brahtchahlehttoa reejeedoa
beads	un rosario	oon rawzarreeoa
bracelet	un braccialetto	oon brachtchahlehttoa
charm bracelet	un ciondolo per braccialetto	oon choandoaloa pair brahtchahlehttoa
brooch	una spilla	oonah speellah
cameo	un cammeo	oon kahmmayoa
chain	una catenina	oonah kahtayneenah
charm	un ciondolo	oon choandoaloa
cigarette case	un portasigarette	oon portahsseegahrayttay
cigarette lighter	un accendino	oon ahtchayndeenoa

clip	un fermaglio	oon fayrmarlyoa
clock	un orologio	oon oaroalojoa
alarm clock	una sveglia	oonah svaylyah
travelling-clock	un orologio da viaggio	oon oaroalojoa dah veeahdjoa
collar stud	un bottoncino da colletto	oon boattoancheenoa dah koallayttoa
cross	una croce	oonah kroachay
cuff-links	dei gemelli	daiee jaymehllee
cutlery	delle posate	dayllay poassartay
earrings	degli orecchini	daylyee oaraykkeenee
jewel box	un portagioielli	oon portahjoeeehllee
manicure set	un completo per manicure	oon koamplaytoa pair mahneekoor
mechanical pencil	una matita a mina cadente	oonah mahteetah ah meenah kahdayntay
necklace	una collana	oonah koallarnah
pendant	un pendente	oon payndayntay
pin	uno spillo	oonoa speelloa
powder compact	un portacipria	oon portahcheepreeah
propelling pencil	una matita a mina cadente	oonah mahteetah ah meenah kahdayntay
ring	un anello	oon ahnehlloa
engagement ring	un anello di fidanzamento	oon ahnehlloa dee feedahntsahmayntoa
signet ring	un anello con sigillo	oon ahnehlloa kon seejeelloa
wedding ring	una fede nuziale	oonah fayday nootsee-arlay
rosary	un rosario	oon rawzarreeoa
silverware	dell'argenteria	dayllahrjayntayreeah
snuff box	una tabacchiera	oonah tahbahkkeeayrah
strap	un cinturino	oon cheentooreenoa
chain strap	a catena	ah kahtaynah
leather strap	di pelle	dee pehllay
watch strap	da orologio	dah oaroalojoa
tie clip	un fermacravatte	oon fayrmahkrahvahttay
tie pin	uno spillo per cravatta	oonoa speelloa pair krahvahttah
vanity case	una borsetta per il trucco	oonah boarsehttah pair eel trookkoa
watch	un orologio	oon oaroalojoa
pocket watch	da tasca	dah tahskah
with a second hand	con lancetta per i secondi	kon lahnchehttah pair ee saykoandee
wristwatch	da polso	dah poalsoa

Laundry – Dry cleaning

If your hotel doesn't have its own laundry or dry cleaning service, ask the porter:

Where's the nearest laundry/dry cleaner's?	**Dov'è la più vicina lavanderia/tintoria ?**	doavai lah peeoo veecheenah lahvahndayreeah/ teentoareeah
I want these clothes…	**Voglio far… questi abiti.**	volyoa farr…kooaystee arbeetee
cleaned	**pulire**	pooleeray
pressed	**stirare (con la pressa)**	steerarray (kon lah prehsssah)
ironed	**stirare**	steerarray
washed	**lavare**	lahvarray
When will it be ready ?	**Quando sarà pronto ?**	kwahndoa sahrah proantoa
I need it…	**Ne ho bisogno…**	nay oa beezoañoa
today	**oggi**	odjee
tonight	**stasera**	stahssayrah
tomorrow	**domani**	doamarnee
before Friday	**prima di venerdì**	preemah dee vaynayrdee
Can you… this ?	**Mi può… questo ?**	mee pwo… kooaystoa
mend	**rammendare**	rahmmayndarray
patch	**rappezzare**	rappehttsarray
stitch	**cucire**	koocheeray
Can you sew on this button ?	**Può attaccare questo bottone ?**	pwo ahttahkkahray kooaystoa boattoanay
Can you get this stain out ?	**Mi può togliere questa macchia ?**	mee pwo tolyayray kooaystah mahkkeeah
Can this be invisibly mended ?	**Mi può fare un rammendo invisibile ?**	mee pwo farray oon rahmmayndoa eenveezeebeelay
This isn't mine.	**Questo non è mio.**	kooaystoa noan ai meeoa
There's one piece missing.	**Manca un capo.**	mahnkah oon karpoa
There's a hole in this.	**C'è un buco in questo.**	chai oon bookoa een kooaystoa
Is my laundry ready ?	**È pronta la mia biancheria ?**	ai prontah lah meeah beeahngkayreeah

Photography

I want an inexpensive camera.	**Voglio una macchina fotografica economica.**	volyoa oonah **mahk**keenah foatoa**grar**feekah aykoa-no**mee**kah
Show me that one in the window.	**Mi faccia vedere quella in vetrina.**	mee **faht**chah vay**day**ray kooay**llah** een vay**tree**nah

Film

Film sizes aren't always indicated the same way in Europe as in the U.S. and Great Britain. Listed below you'll find some equivalents and translations which will be useful.

I'd like a...	**Vorrei...**	vor**raie**
cartridge	**un rotolo**	oon **ro**toaloa
film for this camera	**una pellicola per questa macchina**	oonah pehl**lee**koalah pair koo**ays**ta **mahk**keenah
a...film	**una pellicola...**	oonah pehl**lee**koalah
120	**sei per sei (6×6)**	sehee pair **se**hee
127	**quattro per quattro (4×4)**	**kwaht**troa pair **kwaht**troa
135	**ventiquattro per trentasei (24×36)**	vaynteek**waht**troa pair trayntahs**se**hee
620	**seicentoventi**	seheechehntoavayntee
8-mm	**otto millimetri**	**ot**toa meel**lee**maytree
super 8	**super otto**	**soo**pair **ot**toa
16-mm	**sedici millimetri**	**say**deechee meel**lee**maytree
20 exposures	**venti pose**	**vayn**tee **poa**zay
36 exposures	**trentasei pose**	trayntahs**se**hee **poa**zay
this ASA/DIN number	**questo numero ASA/DIN**	koo**ays**toa **noo**mayroa **ar**sah/deen
fast	**rapido**	**rar**peedoa
fine grain	**a grana fine**	ah **grar**nah **fee**nay
black and white	**bianco e nero**	bee**ahng**koa ay **nay**roa
colour	**a colori**	ah koa**loa**ree
colour negative	**negativo a colori**	naygah**tee**voa ah koa**loa**ree
colour slide	**diapositive a colori**	deeahpoa**zee**teevay ah koa**loa**ree
artificial light type (indoor)	**per luce artificiale**	pair **loo**chay ahrteefee-**char**lay
daylight type (outdoor)	**per luce naturale**	pair **loo**chay nahtoo**rar**lay
Does the price include processing?	**Nel prezzo è incluso lo sviluppo?**	nayl **preht**tsoa ai eeng-**kloo**zoa loa svee**loop**poa

FOR NUMBERS, see page 175

Processing

How much do you charge for developing?	Quanto fate pagare per lo sviluppo?	kwahntoa fartay pahgarray pair loa sveelooppoa
I want... prints of each negative.	Voglio... stampe per ogni negativa.	volyoa... stahmpay pair oañee naygahteevah
with a mat finish with a glossy finish	su carta opaca su carta lucida	soo kahrtah oaparkah soo kahrtah loocheedah
Will you please enlarge this?	Mi può ingrandire questo, per favore?	mee pwo eenggrahndeeray kooaystoa pair fahvoaray
When will it be ready?	Quando sarà pronto?	kwahndoa sahrah prontoa

Accessories and repairs

I want a/some...	Voglio...	volyoa
flash bulbs/cubes	delle lampadine/dei cubi per il flash	dayllay lahmpahdeenay/ daiee koobee pair eel "flash"
for black and white	per bianco e nero	pair beeahngkoa ay nayroa
for colour	per foto a colori	pair foatoa ah koaloaree
filter	un filtro	oon feeltroa
red/yellow	rosso/giallo	roasssoa/jahlloa
Can you repair this camera?	Può riparare questa macchina fotografica?	pwo reepahrarray kooaystah mahkkeenah foatoagrarfeekah
The film is jammed.	La pellicola è bloccata.	lah pehlleekoalah ai bloakkartah
There's something wrong with the...	...è rotto (rotta).	...ai roattoa (roattah)
exposure counter	il contatore di esposizioni	eel koantahtoaray dee ayspoazeetseeoaanee
film winder	la leva d'avanzamento della pellicola	lah layvah dahvahntsahmayntoa dayllah pehlleekoalah
flash attachment	l'attaccatura del flash	lahttahkkahtoorah dayl "flash"
lens	l'obiettivo	loabeeaytteevoa
light meter	l'esposimetro	layspoazeemaytroa
rangefinder	il telemetro	eel taylaymaytroa
shutter	l'otturatore	loattoorahtoaray

Provisions

Here's a basic list of food and drink that you might want on a picnic or for the occasional meal at home:

I'd like a/an/some…, please. **Per favore, vorrei…** pair fahvoaray vorraiee

apples	**delle mele**	dayllay maylay
bananas	**delle banane**	dayllay bahnarnay
biscuits (Br.)	**dei biscotti**	daiee beeskoattee
bread	**del pane**	dayl parnay
butter	**del burro**	dayl boorroa
cake	**un dolce**	oon doalchay
candy	**dei dolciumi**	daiee doalchoomee
cheese	**del formaggio**	dayl foarmahdjoa
chocolate	**della cioccolata**	dayllah chokkoalartah
coffee	**del caffè**	dayl kahffai
cold cuts	**degli affettati**	daylyee ahffehttartee
cookies	**dei biscotti**	daiee beeskoattee
cooking fat	**del grasso per cucinare**	dayl grahsssoa pair koocheenarray
cream	**della crema**	dayllah kraimah
crisps	**delle patatine fritte**	dayllay pahtahteenay freettay
cucumbers	**dei cetrioli**	daiee chaytreeoolee
eggs	**delle uova**	dayllay ooawvah
flour	**della farina**	dayllah fahreenah
frankfurters	**dei Würstel**	daiee "würstel"
ham	**del prosciutto**	dayl proashoottoa
hamburgers	**degli hamburger**	daylyee ahmboorgayr
ice-cream	**un gelato**	oon jaylartoa
lemons	**dei limoni**	daiee leemoanee
lettuce	**della lattuga**	dayllah lahttoogah
luncheon meat	**una salsiccia**	oonah sahlseetchah
milk	**del latte**	dayl lahttay
mustard	**della mostarda**	dayllah moastahrdah
oranges	**delle arance**	dayllay ahrahnchay
peppers	**dei peperoni**	daiee paypayroanee
pickles	**dei sottaceti**	daiee soattahchaytee
potato chips	**delle patatine fritte**	dayllay pahtahteenay freettay
potatoes	**delle patate**	dayllay pahtartay
rolls	**dei panini**	daiee pahneenee
salad	**dell'insalata**	daylleensahlartah
salami	**del salame**	dayl sahlamay
salt	**del sale**	dayl sarlay

sandwiches	**dei sandwich**	daiee "sandwich"
sausages	**delle salsicce**	dayllay sahlseetchay
soft drink	**una bibita**	oonah beebeetah
spaghetti	**degli spaghetti**	daylyee spahgehttee
sugar	**dello zucchero**	daylloa tsookkayroa
sweets	**dei dolciumi**	daiee doalchoomee
tea	**del tè**	dayl tay
tomatoes	**dei pomidoro**	daiee poameedawroa

And don't forget...

a bottle opener	**un apribottiglia**	oon ahpreebotteelyah
a corkscrew	**un cavatappi**	oon kahvahtahppee
matches	**dei fiammiferi**	daiee feeahmmeefayree
(paper) napkins	**dei tovaglioli (di carta)**	daiee toavahlyolee (dee kahrtah)
a tin (can) opener	**un apriscatole**	oon ahpreeskahtoalay

Weights and measures

1 kilogram or kilo (kg) = 1000 grams (g)

| 100 g = 3.5 oz. | ½ kg = 1.1 lb. |
| 200 g = 7.0 oz. | 1 kg = 2.2 lb. |

1 oz. = 28.35 g
1 lb. = 453.60 g

---

1 litre (l) = 0.88 imp. quarts = 1.06 U.S. quarts

| 1 imp. quart = 1.14 l | 1 U.S. quart = 0.95 l |
| 1 imp. gallon = 4.55 l | 1 U.S. gallon = 3.8 l |

---

barrel	**un barile**	oon barreelay
box	**una scatola**	oonah skahtoalah
can	**una latta**	oonah lahttah
carton	**una stecca**	oonah staykkah
crate	**una cassa**	oonah kahsssah
jar	**un vaso**	oon varzoa
packet	**un sacchetto**	oon sahkkehttoa
tin	**una latta**	oonah lahttah
tube	**un tubo**	oon tooboa

Souvenirs

Italy is particularly noted for its top fashion for both men and women. You'll find numerous smart shops and boutiques in major cities, some of which specialize in custom-made clothing like blouses and shirts. Articles made of silk are of a high quality.

Hand-fashioned jewelry made of amber, gold, silver and tortoise shell as well as cameos are particularly appreciated. Often depending upon the region, you'll come upon fine articles made of leather, olivewood or straw or embroidered clothing and accessories.

antiques	**antichità**	ahnteekeetah
ceramics	**ceramica**	chayrarmeekah
doll	**bambola**	bahmboalah
flask of chianti	**fiasco di chianti**	feearskoa dee keeahntee
glassware	**articoli di vetro**	ahrteekoalee dee vehtroa
high fashion	**alta moda**	ahltah modah
jewelry	**gioielli**	joeeehllee
knitwear	**maglieria**	mahlyayreeah
leather work	**pelletteria**	payllayttayreeah
needlework	**ricamo**	reekarmao
porcelain	**porcellana**	poarchayllarnah
shoes	**scarpe**	skahrpay
silk	**seta**	saitah
toys	**giocattoli**	joakahttoalee
woodwork	**lavoro in legno**	lahvoaroa een lehñoa

In Switzerland, you'll find a vast array of watches at prices often well below those at home. An export certificate will save you duty on gold watches or jewelry valued at over 500 francs. The Swiss are also noted for their ceramics, embroidered and handwoven textiles, music boxes and wood carvings.

chocolate	**cioccolato**	choakkoalartoa
cuckoo clock	**orologio a cucù**	oaroalojoa ah kookoo
earthen pitcher	**boccalino**	boakkahleenoa
linen	**biancheria**	beeahngkayreeah
ski equipment	**equipaggiamento da sci**	aykooeepahdjahmayntoa dah shee
watch	**orologio**	oaroalojoa

Tobacconist's

Cigarettes can be bought at the *Sali e Tabacchi* shops, indicated by a sign showing a silver T on a black background.

As at home, cigarettes are generally referred to by their brand names: *Nazionali, Esportazione, Macedonia,* etc. These brands are locally manufactured and quite cheap. Foreign cigarettes are heavily taxed and therefore expensive.

Buying

Give me a/some..., please.	**Per favore, mi dia...**	pair fahvoaray mee deeah
box of...	**una scatola di...**	oonah skahtoalah dee
chewing tobacco	**del tabacco da masticare**	dayl tahbahkkoa dah mahsteekarray
cigar	**un sigaro**	oon seegahroa
cigars	**dei sigari**	daiee seegahree
cigarette case	**un portasigarette**	oon portahsseegahrayttay
cigarette holder	**un bocchino**	oon boakkeenoa
flints	**delle pietrine**	dayllay peeaytreenay
lighter	**un accendino**	oon ahtchayndeenoa
lighter fluid/gas	**della benzina/del gaz per accendino**	dayllah bayndzeenah/dayl gahz pair ahtchayndeenoa
refill for a lighter	**un ricambio per accendino**	oon reekahmbeeoa pair ahtchayndeenoa
matches	**dei fiammiferi**	daiee feeahmmeefayree
packet of cigarettes	**un pacchetto di sigarette**	oon pahkkayttoa dee seegahrayttay
packet of...	**un pacchetto di...**	oon pahkkayttoa dee
pipe	**una pipa**	oonah peepah
pipe cleaners	**dei nettapipe**	daiee nayttahpeepay
pipe rack	**un portapipe**	oon portahpeepay
pipe tobacco	**del tabacco da pipa**	dayl tahbahkkoa dah peepah
pipe tool	**gli arnesi da pipa**	lyee ahrnayssee dah peepah
snuff	**del tabacco da fiuto**	dayl tahbahkkoa dah feeootoa
tobacco pouch	**una borsa per tabacco**	oonah boarsah pair tahbahkkoa
wick	**uno stoppino**	oonoa stoappeenoa

Do you have any...?	**Avete...?**	ahvaytay
American cigarettes	**sigarette americane**	seegahrayttay ahmayree-karnay
English cigarettes	**sigarette inglesi**	seegahrayttay eengglayssee
menthol cigarettes	**sigarette alla menta**	seegahrayttay ahllah mayntah
I'll take two packets.	**Ne prendo due pacchetti.**	nay prehndoa dooay pahkkayttee
I'd like a carton.	**Ne vorrei una stecca.**	nay vorraiee oonah staykkah

filter tipped	**con filtro**	kon feeltroa
without filter	**senza filtro**	sayntsah feeltroa
king-size	**formato lungo**	foarmartoa loonggoa

While we're on the subject of cigarettes, suppose you want to offer somebody one?

Would you like a cigarette?	**Vuole una sigaretta?**	vwawlay oonah seegah-rayttah
Have one of mine.	**Ne prenda una delle mie.**	nay prehndah oonah dayllay meeay
Try one of these.	**Provi una di queste.**	provee oonah dee kooaystay
They're very mild.	**Sono molto leggere.**	soanoa moaltoa laydjayray
They're a bit strong.	**Sono un po' forti.**	soanoa oon po fortee

And if somebody offers you one?

Thank you.	**Grazie.**	grartseeay
No, thanks.	**No, grazie.**	noa grartseeay
I don't smoke.	**Non fumo.**	noan foomoa
I've given it up.	**Ho smesso.**	oa smaysssoa

Your money: banks — currency

Italy's monetary unit is the *lira* (**lee**rah), plural *lire* (**lee**ray), which is actually divided into 100 *centesimi* though you'll never encounter such a petty sum of money.

As there's a shortage of coinage, sales clerks and cashiers may want to give you the correct change by handing you a few telephone tokens or some sweets.

In Italy, banks are open from 8.30 a.m. to 1.30 p.m. They're closed on Saturdays, Sundays and public holidays. In most important airports and railway stations, banks and currency-exchange offices remain open day and night. Also, the banking hours mentioned here may vary according to the season and the region where you are.

Swiss banks are open from 8 to noon and from 2 to 4 p.m. In the larger cities, you'll find currency-exchange offices *(cambio)* which are open outside the normal hours. The Swiss monetary unit is the *franco* (**frahng**koa), plural *franchi* (**frahng**kee), divided into 100 *centesimi* (chehn**tay**zeemee).

When you go to a bank, remember to take your passport with you as you may need it.

Where's the nearest bank?	**Dov'è la banca più vicina?**	doavai lah **bahng**kah peeoo veecheenah
Where can I cash a traveller's cheque (check)?	**Dove posso cambiare un traveller's cheque?**	doavay posssoa kahmbeearray oon "traveller's cheque"
Where's the Banca del Lavoro?	**Dov'è la Banca del Lavoro?**	doavai lah **bahng**kah dayl lahvoaroa

Inside

I want to change some dollars.	**Desidero cambiare dei dollari.**	dayzeedayroa kahmbeearray **daiee dollahree**
I'd like to change some pounds.	**Vorrei cambiare delle sterline.**	vorraiee kahmbeearray **dayllay** stayrleenay

Here's my passport.	Ecco il mio passaporto.	ehkkoa eel meeoa pahsssahportoa
What's the exchange rate?	Qual'è il corso del cambio?	kwahlai eel koarsoa dayl kahmbeeoa
What rate of commission do you charge?	Quanto trattiene di commissione?	kwahntoa trahtteeaynay dee koammeessseeoanay
Can you cash a personal cheque?	Può cambiare un assegno personale?	pwo kahmbeearray oon ahsssayñoa payrsoanarlay
How long will it take to clear?	Quanto tempo ci vorrà per svincolarlo?	kwahntoa tehmpoa chee voarrah pair sveengkoalahrloa
Can you wire my bank in London?	Può telegrafare alla mia banca a Londra?	pwo taylaygrahfarray ahllah meeah bahngkah ah loandrah
I have...	Ho...	oa
a letter of credit	una lettera di credito	oonah lehttayrah dee kraydeetoa
an introduction from...	una lettera di presentazione di...	oonah lehttayrah dee prayzayntahtseeoanay dee
a credit card	una carta di credito	oonah kahrtah dee kraydeetoa
I'm expecting some money from London. Has it arrived yet?	Aspetto del denaro da Londra. È arrivato?	ahspehttoa dayl daynarroa dah loandrah. ai ahrreevartoa
Please give me... notes (bills) and some small change.	Per favore, mi dia... banconote e della moneta.	pair fahvoaray mee deeah... bahngkoanotay ay dayllah moanaytah
Give me... large notes and the rest in small notes.	Mi dia... in grossi tagli ed il resto in piccoli tagli.	mee deeah... een grosssee tahlyee ayd eel rehstoa een peekkoalee tahlyee
Could you please check that again?	Può verificare di nuovo questo?	pwo vayreefeekarray dee nwawvoa kooaystoa

Depositing

| I want to credit this to my account. | Desidero accreditare questo sul mio conto. | dayzeedayroa ahkkraydeetarray kooaystoa sool meeoa koantoa |

| I want to credit this to Mr...'s account. | **Desidero accreditare questo sul conto del signor...** | dayzeedayroa ahkkraydeetarray kooaystoa sool koantoa dayl seefioar |
| Where should I sign? | **Dove devo firmare?** | doavay dayvoa feermarray |

Currency converter

In a world of fluctuating currencies, we can offer no more than this do-it-yourself chart. You can get a card showing current exchange rates from banks, travel agents and tourist offices. Why not fill in this chart, too, for handy reference?

Italy	£	$
10 lire		
50 lire		
75 lire		
100 lire		
500 lire		
1,000 lire		
10,000 lire		
Switzerland	£	$
10 centesimi		
50 centesimi		
1 franco		
2 franchi		
5 franchi		
10 franchi		
100 franchi		
500 franchi		

FOR NUMBERS, see page 175

At the post-office

Post-offices in Italy are open from 8.15 a.m. to 2 p.m. (central post-offices: 8.15 a.m. to 4 p.m.). Swiss post-offices are open from 7.30 to noon and from 1.45 to 6.30 p.m. They're closed on Saturday afternoons in both countries.

Stamps may be obtained from post-offices and *Sali e Tabacchi* shops in Italy; in Switzerland, from post-offices and automatic stamp dispensers.

Where's the nearest post-office?	**Dov'è l'ufficio postale più vicino?**	doavai looffeechoa poastarlay peeoo veecheenoa
Can you tell me how to get to the post-office?	**Può dirmi come arrivare all'ufficio postale?**	pwo deermee koamay ahrreevarray ahllooffeechoa poastarlay
What time does the post-office open/close?	**A che ora apre/chiude l'ufficio postale?**	ah kay oarah arpray/keeooday looffeechoa poastarlay
What window do I go to for stamps?	**A quale sportello devo rivolgermi per i francobolli?**	ah kwahlay spoartehlloa dayvoa reevoljayrmee pair ee frahngkoaboallee
At which counter can I cash an international money order?	**A quale cassa posso riscuotere un vaglia internazionale?**	ah kwahlay kahsssah poasssoa reeskoootayray oon varlyah eentayr-nahtseeoanarlay
I want some stamps, please.	**Desidero dei franco-bolli, per favore.**	dayzeedayroa daiee frahng-koaboallee pair fahvoaray
I want...30-lire stamps and...50-lire stamps.	**Desidero...franco-bolli da 30 lire e... da 50 lire.**	dayzeedayroa...frahngkoa-boallee dah 30 leeray ay...dah 50 leeray
What's the postage for a letter to London?	**Qual'è l'affranca-tura per una lettera per Londra?**	kwahlai lahffrahngkahtoo-rah pair oonah lehttayrah pair loandrah
What's the postage for a postcard to Los Angeles?	**Qual'è l'affranca-tura per una cartoli-na per Los Angeles?**	kwahlai lahffrahngkahtoo-rah pair oonah kahrtoa-eenah pair Los Angeles
Do all letters go airmail?	**Le lettere vanno per via aerea?**	lay lehttayray vahnnoa pair veeah ahayrayah

I want to send this parcel.	**Vorrei spedire questo pacchetto.**	vorraiee spay**dee**ray kooaystoa pahkkehttoa
Where's the mailbox?	**Dov'è la cassetta delle lettere?**	doavai lah kahsssehttah dayllay lehttayray
I want to send this by...	**Desidero inviare questo per...**	dayzeedayroa eenveearray kooaystoa pair
airmail	**via aerea**	veeah ahayrayah
express (special delivery)	**espresso**	aysprehsssoa
registered mail	**raccomandata**	rahkkoamahndartah
Where's the poste restante (general delivery)?	**Dov'è lo sportello del fermo posta?**	doavai loa spoartehlloa dayl fayrmoa postah
Is there any mail for me? My name is...	**C'è della posta per me? Mi chiamo...**	chai dayllah postah pair may? mee keearmoa

FRANCOBOLLI	STAMPS
PACCHI	PARCELS
VAGLIA POSTALI	MONEY ORDERS

Telegrams

In Italy and Switzerland, you'll have to go to the post-office to send a telegram. Some telegraph offices are open 24 hours a day.

I want to send a telegram. May I please have a form?	**Vorrei inviare un telegramma. Può darmi un modulo?**	vorraiee eenveearray oon taylaygrahmmah. pwo darrmee oon modooloa
How much is it per word?	**Quanto costa ogni parola?**	kwahntoa kostah oñee pahrolah
How long will a cable to Boston take?	**Quanto tempo ci vorrà per inviare un telegramma a Boston?**	kwahntoa tehmpoa chee vorrah pair eenveearray oon taylaygrahmmah ah boston
I'd like to reverse the charges.	**Vorrei mandarlo a carico del destinatario.**	vorraiee mahndahrloa ah karreekoa dayl daysteenahtarreeoa

Telephoning

In Italy there are fewer public telephones in the streets than you may be used to. Most people use the public telephone that can be found in cafés and bars. Ask the cashier for tokens *(gettoni)*.

Dialling is straightforward and on an inter-city basis (for large towns). You'll find dialling (area) codes in the directory. If you want to make a long-distance call, you'll have to order it in advance.

I'd like a telephone token.	**Vorrei un gettone telefonico.**	vorraiee oon jayttoanay taylayfoneekoa
Where's the telephone?	**Dov'è il telefono?**	doavai eel taylayfoanoa
Where's the nearest telephone booth?	**Dov'è la cabina telefonica più vicina?**	doavai la kahbeenah taylayfoneekah peeoo veecheenah
May I use your phone?	**Posso usare il suo telefono?**	posssoa oozarray eel soooa taylayfoanoa
Do you have a telephone directory for Rome?	**Ha un elenco telefonico di Roma?**	ah oon aylayngkoa taylayfoneekoa dee roamah
Can you help me get this number?	**Mi può aiutare ad ottenere questo numero?**	mee pwo ighootarray ahd oattaynayray kooaystoa noomayroa

Operator

Do you speak English?	**Parla inglese?**	pahrlah eengglayssay
Good morning, I want Venice 12 34 56.	**Buongiorno. Desidero il 12 34 56 di Venezia.**	bwonjoarnoa. dayzeedayroa eel 12 34 56 dee vaynaitseeah

Note: Numbers are given in pairs.

Can I dial direct?	**Posso chiamare direttamente?**	posssoa keeahmarray deerehttahmayntay
I want to place a personal (person-to-person) call.	**Vorrei fare una telefonata con preavviso.**	vorraiee farray oonah taylayfoanartah kon prayahvveezoa

FOR NUMBERS, see page 175

| I want to reverse the charges. | **Vorrei fare una telefonata con tassa a carico del destinatario.** | vorraiee farray oonah taylayfoanartah kon **tahsssah** ah karreekoa dayl daysteenah**tarreeoa** |
| Will you tell me the cost of the call afterwards? | **Vuol dirmi il costo della telefonata, dopo?** | vwawl **deer**mee eel kostoa dayllah taylayfoanartah **daw**poa |

Telephone alphabet

A	**Ancona**	ahngkoanah	N	**Napoli**	narpoalee
B	**Bari**	barree	O	**Otranto**	oatrahntoa
C	**Catania**	kahtarneeah	P	**Palermo**	pahlehrmoa
D	**Domodossola**	doamoa**doss**soalah	Q	**cu**	koo
E	**Empoli**	aympoalee	R	**Roma**	roamah
F	**Firenze**	feerehntsay	S	**Sassari**	sarsssahree
G	**Genova**	jainoavah	T	**Torino**	tawreenoa
H	**Hotel**	oatehl	U	**Udine**	oodeenay
I	**Imperia**	eempayreeah	V	**Venezia**	vaynaitseeah
J	**i lunga**	ee loonggah	W	**v doppia**	vee doappeeah
K	**kappa**	kahppah	X	**ix**	eekss
L	**Livorno**	leevoarnoa	Y	**i greca**	ee graykah
M	**Milano**	meelarnoa	Z	**zeta**	dzaitah

Speaking

Hello. This is... speaking.	**Pronto. Qui parla...**	prontoa. kooee pahrlah
I want to speak to...	**Vorrei parlare con...**	vorraiee pahrlarray kon
Would you put me through to...?	**Mi vuol mettere in comunicazione con...?**	mee vwawl **mayt**tayray een komooneekahtseeoanay kon
I want extension...	**Mi dia la linea interna...**	mee **dee**ah lah **lee**nayah eentehrnah
Is that...?	**Parlo con...?**	**pahr**loa kon

Bad luck

| Would you please try again later? | **Per favore, vuol provare di nuovo più tardi?** | pair fah**voa**ray vwawl proavarray dee nwawvoa peeoo **tahr**dee |

| Operator, you gave me the wrong number. | **Signorina, mi ha dato il numero sbagliato.** | seeñoareenah mee ah dartoa eel noomayroa zbahlyartoa |
| Operator, we were cut off. | **Signorina, la comunicazione si è interrotta.** | seeñoareenah lah komooneekahtseeoanay see ai eentehrroattah |

Not there

When will he/she be back?	**Quando sarà di ritorno?**	kwahndoa sahrah dee reetoarnoa
Will you tell him/her I called? My name's...	**Vuol dirgli/dirle che ho telefonato? Mi chiamo...**	vwawl deerlyee/deerlay kay oa taylayfoanartoa mee keearmoa
Would you ask him/her to call me?	**Può chiedergli/chiederle di telefonarmi?**	pwo keeaidayrlyee/keeaidayrlay dee taylayfoanarrmee
Would you please take a message?	**Per favore, può trasmettere un messaggio?**	pair fahvoaray pwo trahzmaytayray oon maysssahdjoa

Charges

| What was the cost of that call? | **Quanto è costata la telefonata?** | kwahntoa ai kostartah lah taylayfoanartah |
| I want to pay for the call. | **Desidero pagare la telefonata.** | dayzeedayroa pahgarray lah taylayfoanartah |

C'è una telefonata per lei.	There's a telephone call for you.
Che numero chiama?	What number are you calling?
La linea è occupata.	The line's engaged.
Non risponde.	There's no answer.
Ha chiamato il numero sbagliato.	You've got the wrong number.
Il telefono non funziona.	The phone is out of order.
Egli/Ella è fuori in questo momento.	He's/She's out at the moment.

The car

Filling station

We'll start this section by considering your possible needs at a filling station. Most of them don't handle major repairs; but apart from providing you with fuel, they may be helpful in solving alls kinds of minor problems.

Where's the nearest filling (service) station?	**Dove si trova la stazione di rifornimento più vicina?**	doavay see trawvah lah stahtseeoanay dee reeforneemayntoa peeoo veecheenah
I want 20 litres of petrol (gas), please.	**Vorrei 20 litri di benzina, per favore.**	vorraiee 20 leetree dee bayndzeenah pair fahvoaray
I want 30 litres of standard/premium.	**Vorrei 30 litri di normale/super.**	vorraiee 30 leetree dee noarmarlay/soopayr
Give me 3,000 lire worth of...	**Vorrei 3.000 lire di...**	vorraiee 3.000 leeray dee
Fill her up, please.	**Il pieno, per favore.**	eel peeainoa pair fahvoaray
Please check the oil and water.	**Per favore, controlli l'olio e l'acqua.**	pair fahvoaray koantroallee lawlyoa ay lahkkwah
Give me 2 litres of oil.	**Mi dia 2 litri di olio.**	mee deeah 2 leetree dee awlyoa
Fill up the battery with distilled water.	**Riempia la batteria con acqua distillata.**	reeaympeeah lah bahttayreeah kon ahkkwah deesteellartah
Check the brake fluid.	**Controlli l'olio dei freni.**	koantroallee lawlyoa daiee frehnee

Fluid measures					
litres	imp. gal.	U.S. gal.	litres	imp. gal.	U.S. gal.
5	1.1	1.3	30	6.6	7.8
10	2.2	2.6	35	7.7	9.1
15	3.3	3.9	40	8.8	10.4
20	4.4	5.2	45	9.9	11.7
25	5.5	6.5	50	11.0	13.0

FOR NUMBERS, see page 175

Tire pressure			
lb. / sq. in.	kg. / cm²	lb. / sq. in.	kg. / cm²
10	0.7	26	1.8
12	0.8	27	1.9
15	1.1	28	2.0
18	1.3	30	2.1
20	1.4	33	2.3
21	1.5	36	2.5
23	1.6	38	2.7
24	1.7	40	2.8

Would you check the tire pressure?	**Può controllare la pressione delle gomme?**	pwo koantroallarray lah praysseoanay **dayl**lay **goam**may
1.6 front, 1.8 rear.	**1,6 davanti, 1,8 dietro.**	1,6 dah**vahn**tee 1,8 dee**eeh**troa
Please check the spare tire, too.	**Per favore, controlli anche la ruota di scorta.**	pair fahvoaray koantroallee **ahng**kay lah rwawtah dee **skor**tah
Can you mend this puncture (fix this flat)?	**Può riparare questa foratura?**	pwo reepahrarray **kooay**stah forah**toor**ah
Would you please change this tire?	**Può cambiarmi la gomma, per favore?**	pwo kahmbeearrmee lah **goam**mah pair fahvoaray
Would you clean the windscreen (windshield)?	**Mi pulisca il parabrezza, per favore.**	mee pooleeskah eel pahrah**brayd**zah pair fahvoaray
Do you have a road map of this district?	**Ha una carta stradale della regione?**	ah **oon**ah **kahr**tah strah**darl**ay **dayl**lah ray**joa**nay
Where are the toilets?	**Dove sono i gabinetti?**	**doa**vay **soa**noa ee gahbee**nayt**tee

* Italians don't say, for instance, one *point* eight but simply one eight or in Italian *uno-otto* (**oo**noa – **ot**toa).

Asking the way – Street directions

Excuse me.	**Mi scusi.**	mee **skoo**zee
Can you tell me the way to…?	**Può dirmi qual'è la strada per…?**	pwo **deer**mee kwah**lai** lah **strar**dah pair
How do I get to…?	**Come si va a…?**	**koa**may see vah ah
Where does this road lead to?	**Dove porta questa strada?**	**doa**vay **por**tah koo**ay**stah **strar**dah
Are we on the right road for…?	**Siamo sulla strada giusta per…?**	see**ar**moa **sool**lah **strar**dah **joo**stah pair
How far is the next village?	**Quanto dista il prossimo villaggio?**	**kwahn**toa **dee**stah eel **pross**seemoa veel**lahd**joa
How far is it to… from here?	**Quanto dista… da qui?**	**kwahn**toa **dee**stah…dah **koo**ee
Can you tell me, where…is?	**Sa dirmi dov'è…?**	sah **deer**mee doa**vai**
Where can I find this address?	**Dove posso trovare questo indirizzo?**	**doa**vay **poss**soa traw**var**ray koo**ay**stoa eendee**reet**tsoa
Where's this?	**Dov'è questo?**	doa**vai** koo**ay**stoa

Miles into kilometres

1 mile = 1.609 kilometres (km.)

miles	10	20	30	40	50	60	70	80	90	100
km.	16	32	48	64	80	97	113	129	145	161

Kilometres into miles

1 kilometre (km. = 0.62 miles)

km.	10	20	30	40	50	60	70	80	90	100	110	120	130
miles	6	12	19	25	31	37	44	50	56	62	68	75	81

Can you show me on the map where I am?	**Può indicarmi sulla carta dove mi trovo?**	pwo eendee**karr**mee soollah **kahr**tah **doa**vay mee **trawv**oa
Can you show me on the map where the university is?	**Può indicarmi sulla carta dove si trova l'università?**	pwo eendee**karr**mee soollah **kahr**tah **doa**vay see **trawv**ah looneevayrseetah
Can I park there?	**Posso parcheggiare là?**	**poss**soa pahrkaydj**ar**ray lah
Is that a one-way street?	**È una strada a senso unico?**	ai oonah **strar**dah ah **sayn**soa **oo**neekoa
Does the traffic go this way?	**La circolazione va in questo senso?**	lah cheerkoalahtseeoanay vah een kooaystoa **sayn**soa

Lei è sulla strada sbagliata.	You're on the wrong road.
Vada diritto.	Go straight ahead.
È laggiù a...	It's down there on the...
sinistra/destra	left/right
Vada fino al primo incrocio.	Go to the first (second) crossroads.
Al semaforo, giri a sinistra.	Turn left at the traffic lights.
Giri a destra al prossimo angolo.	Turn right at the next corner.

CAR—INFORMATION

In the rest of this section we'll be more closely concerned with the car itself. We've divided it into two parts:

Part A contains general advice on motoring in Italy and Switzerland. It's essentially for reference and is therefore to be browsed over, preferably in advance.

Part B is concerned with the practical details of accidents and breakdown. It includes a list of car parts and a list of things that may go wrong with them. All you have to do is to show it to the garage mechanic and get him to point to the items required.

Part A

Customs – Documentation

You'll need the following documents when driving in Italy:

passport
international insurance certificate (green card)
registration (log) book
valid driving licence

The nationality plate or sticker must be on the car. Since some countries require a translation of your home driving licence, an international driving permit may save you trouble.

A red warning triangle – for display on the road in case of accident – is compulsory; parking lights are advisable. Crash helmets are mandatory for both riders and passengers on motorcycles and scooters.

Here's my...	Ecco...	ehkkoa
driving licence	**la patente**	lah pahtehntay
green card	**la carta verde**	lah kahrtah vayrday
passport	**il passaporto**	eel pahsssahportoa
registration book	**il libretto di iscrizione**	eel leebrehttoa dee eeskreetseeoanay
I have nothing to declare.	**Non ho nulla da dichiarare.**	noan oa noollah dah deekeeahrarray

I've...	Ho...	oa
a carton of cigarettes	**una stecca di sigarette**	oonah **stayk**kah dee seegah**rayt**tay
a bottle of whisky	**una bottiglia di whisky**	oonah bott**ee**lyah dee whisky
a bottle of wine	**una bottiglia di vino**	oonah bott**ee**lyah dee **vee**noa
We're staying for...	**Resteremo...**	raystayray**moa**
a week	**una settimana**	oonah saytteemar**nah**
ten days	**dieci giorni**	deeaichee **joar**nee
a fortnight (two weeks)	**due settimane**	dooay saytteemar**nay**
a month	**un mese**	oon **mais**say

Driving

The classification of roads in Italy is as follows:

Autostrada	Motorway (expressway). Italy has an extensive network of motorways covering the entire country. A toll is charged according to the distance you want to travel. Sign posts indicating the way to a motorway are green.
S. S. 5	*Strada Statale*—first-class main road
S. P. 3	*Strada Provinciale*—second-class through road

The smaller roads, the *strada comunale* for example, vary greatly in quality from region to region.

The traffic regulations valid in Italy and Switzerland are generally the same as those observed in most other European countries. But remember – drive on the right, overtake on the left. Trams have priority over all other vehicles. Unless otherwise indicated, traffic coming from the right always has priority over traffic going straight on.

Horns should be used with moderation, especially at night and near populated areas; however, you'll notice that the Italians themselves don't always seem to have heard about this rule. Outside city limits, it's obligatory to use the direction indicators (turn signals) when overtaking, when changing lanes and when starting from a halt. You may dial 116 from any place in Italy for emergency road assistance.

The police are normally quite lenient with tourists, but don't push your luck too far. For small offences you can be fined on the spot. Here are some phrases which may come in handy in case of confrontation with the *Polizia* or the *Carabinieri*. If you're in serious trouble, insist on an interpreter.

I'm sorry, I didn't see the sign.	**Mi dispiace, non ho visto il segnale.**	mee deespeearchay noan oa veestoa eel sayñarlay
The light was green.	**Il semaforo era verde.**	eel saymarfoaroa ayrah vayrday
I'm sorry, I don't speak Italian very well.	**Mi dispiace, non parlo bene l'italiano.**	mee deespeearchay noan pahrloa bainay leetahleearnoa
How much is the fine?	**Quant'è la multa?**	kwahntai lah mooltah

Parking

Use your common sense when parking. Park your vehicle in the direction of moving traffic, not against it. Obey the parking regulations which will be indicated by signs or by lines painted on the kerb (curb).

Excuse me. May I park here?	**Mi scusi, posso parcheggiare qui?**	mee skoozee posssoa pahrkaydjarray kooee
How long can I park here?	**Per quanto tempo posso parcheggiare qui?**	pair kwahntoa tehmpoa posssoa pahrkaydjarray kooee
Do I have to leave my lights on?	**Devo lasciare accese le luci?**	dayvoa lahsharray ahtchayzay lay loochee
Excuse me. Do you have some change for the parking meter?	**Mi scusi, ha la moneta per il contatore del parcheggio?**	mee skoozee ah lah moanaytah pair eel koantahtoaray dayl pahrkaydjoa

Road signs

Road signs are practically standardized throughout Western Europe. You should learn to recognize them, particularly those shown on pages 160 and 161.

Listed below are some written signs which you'll certainly encounter when driving in Italy or Switzerland. Obviously, they should be studied in advance. You can't drive and read at the same time!

ACCENDERE I FARI IN GALLERIA	Use headlights before entering tunnel
ACCOSTARE A DESTRA (SINISTRA)	Keep right (left)
ALT	Stop
AREA DI SERVIZIO	Service area
AVANTI	Walk
CADUTA MASSI	Falling rocks
CARABINIERI	Police
CIRCONVALLAZIONE	Ring road (belt highway)
CORSIA D'EMERGENZA	Emergency parking zone
CURVE PER 5 KM.	Bends (curves) for 5 km.
DEVIAZIONE	Diversion/detour
DIVIETO DI SOSTA	No parking
DIVIETO DI SORPASSO	No overtaking (passing)
DOGANA	Customs
LAVORI IN CORSO	Road works ahead (men working)
PAGAMENTO PEDAGGIO	Toll
PARCHEGGIO SOCI A.C.I.	Parking reserved for A.C.I.
PASSAGGIO A LIVELLO	Level (railroad) crossing
PASSAGGIO SCOLARI	School crossing
PERICOLO	Danger
POLIZIA STRADALE	Highway police
RALLENTARE	Reduce speed
SEMAFORI SINCRONIZZATI	Synchronized traffic lights
SENSO UNICO	One way
SILENZIO	Silence
SOCCORSO A.C.I.	A.C.I. emergency road service
SORPASSO	Lane for overtaking (passing)
TRANSITO CON CATENE	Chains required
VICOLO CIECO	Dead end
VIETATO L'ACCESSO	No entry
VIGILI URBANI	City police
ZONA PEDONALE	Pedestrian zone

Part B

Accidents

This section is confined to immediate aid. The legal problems of responsibility and settlement can be taken care of at a later stage.

Your first concern will be for the injured.

Is anyone hurt?	**Vi sono dei feriti?**	vee soanoa daiee fayreetee
Don't move.	**Non si muova.**	noan see mwawvvah
It's all right. Don't worry.	**Va tutto bene. Non si preoccupi.**	vah toottoa bainay. noan see prayoakkoopee
Where's the nearest telephone?	**Dov'è il telefono più vicino?**	doavai eel taylayfoanoa peeoo veecheenoa
Can I use your telephone? There's been an accident.	**Posso usare il suo telefono? C'è stato un incidente.**	posssoa oozarray eel soooa taylayfonoa? chai startoa oon eencheedayntay
Call a doctor/an ambulance quickly	**Chiami un dottore/un'autoambulanza, presto.**	keearmee oon doattoaray/oonowtoaahmboolahntsah prehstoa
There are people injured.	**Ci sono dei feriti.**	chee soanoa daiee fayreetee
Help me get them out of the car.	**Mi aiuti ad estrarli dalla macchina.**	mee ighootee ahd aystrahrlee dahllah mahkkeenah

Police – Exchange of information

Please call the police.	**Per favore, chiami la polizia.**	pair fahvoaray keearmee lah poaleetseeah
There's been an accident. It's about 2 km. from...	**C'è stato un incidente. È a circa 2 chilometri da...**	chai startoa oon eencheedayntay. ai ah cheerkah 2 keelomaytree dah
I'm on the Florence-Bologna road, 25 km. from Bologna.	**Sono sulla strada Firenze-Bologna, 25 chilometri da Bologna.**	soanoa soollah strardah feerehntsay-boaloañah 25 keelomaytree dah boaloañah
Here's my name and address.	**Ecco il mio nome e indirizzo.**	ehkkoa eel meeoa nomay ay eendeereettsoa

CAR–INFORMATION

Would you mind acting as a witness?	**Le spiacerebbe fare da testimone?**	lay speeahchayrehbbay farray dah taysteemonay
I'd like an interpreter.	**Vorrei un interprete.**	vorraiee oon eentehr-praytay

Remember to put out a red triangle warning if the car is out of action or impeding traffic.

Breakdown

...and that's what we'll do with this section: break it down into four phases.

1. *On the road*
   You ask where the nearest garage is.

2. *At the garage*
   You tell the mechanic what's wrong.

3. *Finding the trouble*
   He tells you what he thinks is wrong.

4. *Getting it repaired*
   You tell him to repair it and, once that's over, settle the account (or argue about it).

Phase 1 – On the road

Where's the nearest garage?	**Dov'è il garage più vicino?**	doavai eel gahrarzh peeoo veecheenoa
Excuse me. My car has broken down. May I use your phone?	**Mi scusi. Ho un guasto all'automobile. Posso usare il suo telefono?**	mee skoozee. oa oon gwarstoa ahllowtoamawbeelay. posssoa oozarray eel soooa taylayfoanoa
What's the telephone number of the nearest garage?	**Qual'è il numero di telefono del garage più vicino?**	kwahlai eel noomayroa dee taylayfoanoa dayl gahrarzh peeoo veecheenoa
I've had a breakdown at...	**Ho avuto un guasto a...**	oa ahvootoa oon gwarstoa ah
We're on the Rome-Naples motorway (expressway), about 10 km. from Naples.	**Siamo sull'autostrada Roma-Napoli a circa 10 chilometri da Napoli.**	seearmoa soollowtoastrardah roamah-narpoalee ah cheerkah 10 keelomaytree dah narpoalee

Can you send a mechanic?	Può mandare un meccanico?	pwo mahndarray oon maykkarneekoa
Can you send a truck to tow my car?	Può mandare un autocarro per rimorchiare la mia macchina?	pwo mahndarray oonowtoakahrroa pair reemoarkeearray lah meeah mahkkeenah
How long will you be?	Quanto tempo impiegherete?	kwahntoa tehmpoa eempeeaygayraytay

Phase 2 – At the garage

Can you help me?	Può aiutarmi?	pwo ighootarrmee
I don't know what's wrong with it.	Non so dove sia il guasto.	noan soa doavay seeah eel gwarstoa
I think there's something wrong with the...	Penso che...non funzioni (funzionino).	paynsoa kay...noan foontseeoanee (foontseeoaneenoa)
battery	la batteria	lah bahttayreeah
brakes	i freni	ee frehnee
bulbs	le lampade	lay lahmpahday
carburettor	il carburatore	eel kahrboorahtoaray
clutch	la frizione	lah freetseeoanay
contact	il contatto	eel koantahttoa
cooling system	il sistema di raffreddamento	eel seestehmah dee rahffrayddahmayntoa
dipswitch (dimmer switch)	il commutatore delle luci	eel koammootahtoaray dayllay loochee
dynamo	la dinamo	lah deenahmoa
electrical system	l'impianto elettrico	leempeeahntoa aylehttreekoa
engine	il motore	eel mawtoaray
exhaust pipe	il tubo di scappamento	eel tooboa dee skahppahmayntoa
fan	il ventilatore	eel vaynteelahtoaray
filter	il filtro	eel feeltroa
fuel pump	la pompa della benzina	lah poampah dayllah bayndzeenah
fuel tank	il serbatoio della benzina	eel sayrbahtoeeoa dayllah bayndzeenah
gears	le marce	lay mahrchay
generator	il generatore	eel jaynayrahtoaray
hand brake	il freno a mano	eel frehnoa ah marnoa
headlights	i fari anteriori	ee farree ahntayreeoaree
heating	il riscaldamento	eel reeskahldahmayntoa
horn	il clacson	eel klaksoan

ignition system	**l'accensione**	lahtchaynseeoanay
indicator	**la freccia di direzione**	lah fraytchah dee deeraytseeoanay
lights	**le luci**	lay loochee
brake	**dei freni**	daiee frehnee
rear (tail)	**posteriori**	poastayreeoaree
reversing (back-up)	**della retromarcia**	dayllah rehtroamahrchah
lining and covering	**la guarnizione e il rivestimento**	lah gwahrneetseeoanay ay eel reevaysteemayntoa
lubrication system	**il sistema di lubrificazione**	eel seestehmah dee loobreefeekahtseeoanay
muffler	**la marmitta di scarico**	lah mahrmeettah dee skarreekoa
parking brake	**il freno a mano**	eel frehnoa ah marnoa
radiator	**il radiatore**	eel rahdeeahtoaray
reflectors	**i catarifrangenti**	ee kahtahreefrahnjayntee
seat	**il sedile**	eel saydeelay
silencer	**il silenziatore**	eel seelayntseeahtoaray
sliding roof	**la capote**	lah kahpot
sparking plugs	**le candele**	lay kahndehlay
speedometer	**il tachimetro**	eel tahkeemaytroa
starter	**il motorino d'avviamento**	eel mawtoareenoa davveeahmayntoa
steering	**il volante**	eel volahntay
suspension	**la sospensione**	lah soaspaynseeoanay
(automatic) transmission	**il cambio (automatico)**	eel kahmbeeoa (owtoamarteekoa)
turn signal	**la freccia di direzione**	lah fraytchah dee deeraytseeoanay
wheels	**le ruote**	lay rwawtay
wipers	**i tergicristalli**	ee tayrjeekreestahllee

RIGHT	LEFT	FRONT	BACK
DESTRA	**SINESTRA**	**DAVANTI**	**DIETRO**
(dehstrah)	(seeneestrah)	(dahvahntee)	(deeaitroa)

It's...	È...	ai
bad	**in cattivo stato**	een kahtteevoa startoa
blown	**strappato**	strahppartoa
broken	**rotto**	roattoa
burnt	**bruciato**	broochartoa
cracked	**incrinato**	eengkreenartoa
defective	**difettoso**	deefehttoassoa

disconnected	disinnestato	deezeennehstartoa
dry	secco	saykkoa
frozen	gelato	jaylartoa
jammed	bloccato	blokkartoa
leaking	fessurato	faysssoorartoa
loose	staccato	stahkkartoa
misfiring	si accende irrego-larmente	see ahtchaynday eerray-goalahrmayntay
noisy	rumoroso	roomoaroassoa
not working	non funziona	noan foontseeoanah
overheating	surriscaldato	soorreeskahldartoa
short circuiting	un corto-circuito	oon koartoa cheer-kooeetoa
slipping	scivolato	sheevoalartoa
stuck	impigliato	eempeelyartoa
weak	debole	daiboalay
worn	consumato	koansoomartoa

The car won't start.	La macchina non parte.	lah mahkkeenah noan pahrtay
It's locked and the keys are inside.	È chiusa a chiave e le chiavi sono all'interno.	ai keeoossah ah keearvay ay lay keearvee soanoa ahlleentehrnoa
The fan belt is too slack.	La cinghia del venti-latore è troppo lenta.	lah cheenggeeah dayl vaynteelahtoaray ai troppoa lehntah
The radiator is leaking.	Il radiatore perde.	eel rahdeeahtoaray pehrday
I want maintenance and lubrication service.	Desidero il servizio di manutenzione e di lubrificazione.	dayzeedayroa eel sayrvee-tseeoa dee mahnootayn-tseeoanay ay dee loobree-feekahtseeoanay
The clutch engages too quickly.	La frizione stacca troppo in fretta.	lah freetseeoanay stahkkah troppoa een frayttah
The steering wheel's vibrating.	Il volante vibra.	eel volahntay veebrah
The wipers are smearing.	I tergicristalli sono imbrattati.	ee tayrjeekreestahllee soanoa eembrahttartee
The pneumatic suspension is weak.	La sospensione pneumatica è debole.	la soaspaynseeoanay pnayoomarteekah ai daiboalay
The brakes needs adjusting.	I freni devono essere aggiustati.	ee frehnee dayvoanoa ehsssayray ahdjoostartee

Now that you've explained what's wrong, you'll want to know how long it'll take to repair it.

How long will it take to repair?	**Quanto tempo ci vorrà per ripararla?**	kwahntoa **tehm**poa chee vorrah pair reepahrahrlah
How long will it take to find out what's wrong?	**Quanto tempo ci vorrà per trovare il guasto?**	kwahntoa **tehm**poa chee vorrah pair troavarray eel gwarstoa
Suppose I come back in half an hour?	**Posso tornare tra mezz'ora?**	**posss**oa toarnarray trah mehd**dzo**arah
Can you give me a lift into town?	**Può darmi un passaggio fino in città?**	pwo **dahr**mee oon pahss-**sahd**joa **fee**noa een cheet**tah**

Phase 3 – Finding the trouble

It's up to the mechanic either to find the trouble or to repair it. All you have to do is hand him the book and point to the text in Italian below.

Per favore, guardi la seguente lista alfabetica ed indichi il pezzo difettoso. Se il cliente vuol sapere perchè non funziona, scelga il termine appropriato dalla lista che segue (è rotto, c'è un corto circuito, ecc.).*

acqua distillata	distilled water
albero	shaft
albero di distribuzione	camshaft
albero motore	crankshaft
ammortizzatore	shock-absorber
aste	stems
basamento	crankcase
batteria	battery
blocco del motore	block
bobina	ignition coil
cambio automatico	automatic transmission
candele	sparking plugs
carburatore	carburettor
cavo	cable
cavi delle candele	sparking-plug leads
cavi dello spinterogeno	distributor leads

* Please look at the following alphabetical list and point to the defective item. If your customer wants to know what's wrong with it, pick the applicable term from the next list (broken, short-circuited, etc.).

CAR—REPAIRS

cilindro	cylinder
cinghia del ventilatore	fan-belt
collegamento	connection
commutatore delle luci	dipswitch (dimmer switch)
condensatore	condensor
contatto	contact
cremagliera e pignone	rack and pinion
cuscinetto	bearing
cuscinetti di banco	main bearings
denti	teeth
diaframma	diaphragm
dinamo	dynamo (generator)
disco della frizione	clutch plate
elementi della batteria	battery cells
fasce elastiche	piston rings
filtro dell'aria	air filter
filtro della benzina	petrol (gas) filter
filtro dell'olio	oil filter
freno	brake
frizione	clutch
galleggiante	float
generatore	dynamo (generator)
giunto	joint
giunto cardanico	universal joint
guarnizione	lining
guarnizione della testa del cilindro	cylinder head gasket
impianto elettrico	electrical system
indotto del motorino d'avviamento	starter armature
molla della valvola	valve spring
molle	springs
molle a pressione	pressure springs
motore	engine
motorino d'avviamento	starter motor
pattini	shoes
pedale della frizione	clutch pedal
piantone dello sterzo	steering column
pistone	piston
pompa	pump
pompa dell'acqua	water pump
pompa della benzina	petrol pump
pompa d'iniezione	injection pump
pompa dell'olio	oil pump
punteria	tappets
puntine platinate	points

radiatore	radiator
rosette	rings
ruote	wheels
scatola dello sterzo	steering box
sistema di raffreddamento	cooling system
sospensione	suspension
sospensione pneumatica	pneumatic suspension
spazzole	brushes
spinterogeno	distributor
stabilizzatore	stabilizer
sterzo	steering
tamburo del freno	brake drum
termostato	thermostat
testa del cilindro	cylinder head
tiranti trasversali	track rod ends
trasmissione	transmission
valvola	valve
ventilatore	fan

Nella seguente lista troverete le parole per descrivere ciò che non funziona e ciò che deve essere fatto.*

aggiustare	to adjust
allentare	to loosen
allentato	slack
alto	high
avvitare	to grind in
basso	low
batte in testa	knocking
bilanciare	to balance
bloccato	jammed
bruciato	burnt/blown
cambiare	to change
caricare	to charge
consumato	worn
corroso	corroded
corto	short
corto circuito	short-circuited
curvato	warped
debole	weak
difettoso	defective
disinnestato	disconnected
foratura	puncture
gelato	frozen

* The following list contains words which describe what's wrong as well as what may need to be done.

guarnire	to reline
impigliato	stuck
incrinato	cracked
mettere in moto	play
non stacca bene	slipping
perde	leaking
pulire	clean
rapido	quick
rotto	broken
sciolto	loose
secco	dry
si accende irregolarmente	misfiring
si surriscalda	overheating
sostituire	to replace
sporco	dirty
spurgare	to bleed
staccare	to strip down
stringere	to tighten
vibra	vibrating

Phase 4 – Getting it repaired

Have you found the trouble?	**Ha trovato il guasto?**	ah troavartoa eel **gwarstoa**

Now that you know what's wrong or at least have some idea, you'll want to find out...

Is that serious?	**È grave?**	ai **grar**vay
Can you repair it?	**Può ripararlo?**	pwo reepahrahrloa
Can you do it now?	**Può farlo subito?**	pwo **fahr**loa soobeetoa
What's it going to cost?	**Quanto costerà?**	kwahntoa kostayrah
Do you have the necessary spare parts?	**Ha i pezzi di ricambio necessari?**	ah ee **peht**tsee dee reekahmbeeoa naychayss-sarree

What if he says "no"?

Why can't you do it?	**Perchè non può farlo?**	pehrkay noan pwo **fahr**loa
Is it essential to have that part?	**È indispensabile avere quel ricambio?**	ai eendeespaynsahbeelay ahvayray kooayl reekahmbeeoa

How long is it going to take to get the spare parts?	Quanto tempo occorre per avere i pezzi di ricambio?	kwahntoa tehmpoa oakkoarray pair ahvayray ee pehttsee dee reekahmbeeoa
Where's the nearest garage that can repair it?	Dov'è il garage più vicino che può riparare il guasto?	doavai eel gahrazh peeoo veecheenoa kay pwo reepahrarray eel gwarstoa
Can you fix it so that I can get as far as...?	Può aggiustarlo in modo che possa andare fino a...?	pwo ahdjoostahrloa een modoa kay posssah ahndarray feenoa ah

If you're really stuck, ask if you can leave the car at the garage. Contact the automobile association or hire another car.

Settling the bill

| Is everything fixed? | Tutto è a posto? | toottoa ai ah poastoa |
| How much do I owe you? | Quanto le devo? | kwahntoa lay dayvoa |

The garage then presents you a bill. If you're satisfied...

Will you take a traveller's cheque?	Accetta un traveller's cheque?	ahtchayttah oon "traveller's cheque"
Thanks very much for your help.	Mille grazie per il suo aiuto.	meellay grartseeay pair eel soooa ighootoa
This is for you.	Questo è per lei.	kooaystoa ai pair laiee

But you may feel that the workmanship is sloppy or that you are paying for work not done. Get the bill itemized. If necessary, get it translated before you pay.

| I'd like to check the bill first. Will you itemize the work done? | Vorrei controllare il conto prima. Vuole specificarmi il lavoro eseguito? | vorraiee koantroallarray eel koantoa preemah. vwolay spaycheefeekahrmee eel lahvoaroa ayzaygooeetoa |

If the garage still won't back down and you're sure you are right, get the help of a third party.

Some international road signs

No vehicles

No entry

No overtaking (passing)

Oncoming traffic has priority

Maximum speed limit

No parking

Caution

Intersection

Dangerous bend (curve)

Road narrows

Intersection with secondary road

Two-way traffic

Dangerous hill

Uneven road

Falling rocks

Give way (yield)

Main road,
thoroughfare

End of restriction

One-way traffic

Traffic goes
this way

Roundabout
(rotary)

Bicycles only

Pedestrians
only

Minimum speed
limit

Keep right
(left if symbol
reversed)

Parking

Hospital

Motorway
(expressway)

Motor vehicles
only

Filling station

No through road

Doctor

Frankly, how much use is a phrase book going to be to you in case of serious injury or illness? The only phrase you need in such an emergency is...

| Get a doctor quickly! | **Chiamate un medico, presto!** | keeahmartay oon maideekoa prehstoa |

But there are minor aches and pains, ailments and irritations that can upset the best planned trip. Here we can help you and, perhaps, the doctor.

Some doctors will speak English well; others will know enough for your needs. But suppose there's something the doctor can't explain because of language difficulties? We've thought of that. As you'll see, this section has been arranged to enable you and the doctor to communicate. From pages 165 to 171, you find your part of the dialogue on the upper half of each page—the doctor's is on the lower half.

The whole section has been divided into three parts: illness, wounds, nervous tension. Page 171 is concerned with prescriptions and fees.

General

I need a doctor quickly.	**Ho bisogno di un medico, presto.**	oa beezoañoa dee oon maideekoa prehstoa
Can you get me a doctor?	**Può chiamarmi un medico?**	pwo keeahmahrmee oon maideekoa
Is there a doctor here?	**C'è un medico qui?**	chai oon maideekoa kooee
Please telephone for a doctor immediately.	**Telefoni subito ad un medico, per favore.**	taylayfoanee soobeetoa ahd oon maideekoa pair fahvoaray
Where's there a doctor who speaks English?	**C'è qui un medico che parla inglese?**	chai kooee oon maideekoa kay pahrlah eengglayssay
Where's the surgery (doctor's office)?	**Dov'è l'ambulatorio del medico?**	doavai lahmboolahtoreeoa dayl maideekoa

What are the surgery (office) hours?	**Quali sono le ore di consultazione?**	kwahlee soanoa lay oaray dee koansooltahtseeoanay
Could the doctor come to see me here?	**Il medico può venire a visitarmi qui?**	eel maideekoa pwo vayneeray ah veezeetahrmee kooee
What time can the doctor come?	**Quando può venire il medico?**	kwahndoa pwo vayneeray eel maideekoa

Symptoms

Use this section to tell the doctor what's wrong. Basically, what he'll require to know is:

What? (ache, pain, bruise, etc.)
Where? (arm, stomach, etc.)
How long? (have you had the trouble)

Before you visit the doctor find out the answers to these questions by glancing through the pages that follow. In this way, you'll save time.

Parts of the body

ankle	**la caviglia**	lah kahveelyah
appendix	**l'appendice**	lahppayndeechay
arm	**il braccio**	eel brahtchoa
artery	**l'arteria**	lahrtaireeah
back	**la schiena**	lah skeeainah
bladder	**la vescica urinaria**	lah vaysheekah ooreenarreeah
blood	**il sangue**	eel sahnggooay
bone	**l'osso**	losssoa
bowels	**le viscere**	lay veeshayray
breast	**il petto**	eel pehttoa
cheek	**la guancia**	lah gwahnchah
chest	**il torace**	eel toararchay
chin	**il mento**	eel mayntoa
collar-bone	**la clavicola**	lah klahveekoalah
ear	**l'orecchio**	loaraykkeeoa
elbow	**il gomito**	eel goameetoa
eye	**l'occhio**	lokkeeoa
eyes	**gli occhi**	lyee okkee
face	**il viso**	eel veezoa
finger	**il dito della mano**	eel deetoa dayllah marnoa

foot	il piede	eel peeayday
forehead	la fronte	lah froantay
gland	la glandola	lah glahndoalah
hair	i capelli	ee kahpayllee
hand	la mano	lah marnoa
head	la testa	lah tehstah
heart	il cuore	eel kworay
heel	il tallone	eel tahlloanay
hip	l'anca	lahngkah
intestines	gli intestini	lyee eentaysteenee
jaw	la mascella	lah mahshehllah
joint	l'articolazione	lahrteekoalahtseeoaanay
kidney	il rene	eel rainay
knee	il ginocchio	eel jeenokkeeoa
knee cap	la rotula	lah rotoolah
leg	la gamba	lah gahmbah
lip	il labbro	eel lahbbroa
liver	il fegato	eel faygahtoa
lung	il polmone	eel poalmoanay
mouth	la bocca	lah boakkah
muscle	il muscolo	eel mooskoaloa
neck	il collo	eel kolloa
nerve	il nervo	eel nehrvoa
nervous system	il sistema nervoso	eel seestaimah nehrvoassoa
nose	il naso	ell narssoa
rib	la costola	lah kostoalah
shoulder	la spalla	lah spahllah
skin	la pelle	lah pehllay
spine	la spina dorsale	lah speenah doarsarlay
stomach	lo stomaco	loa stomahkoa
tendon	il tendine	eel tehndeenay
thigh	la coscia	lah koshah
throat	la gola	lah goalah
thumb	il pollice	eel polleechay
toe	il dito del piede	eel deetoa dayl peeayday
tongue	la lingua	lah leenggwah
tonsils	le tonsille	lay toanseellay
urine	l'urina	looreenah
vein	la vena	lah vaynah
wrist	il polso	eel poalsoa

left/on the left side	right/on the right side
sinistro/a sinistra	**destro/a destra**
(seeneestroa/ah seeneestrah)	(dehstroa/ah dehstrah)

PATIENT

Part 1 — Illness

I'm not feeling well.	**Non mi sento bene.**	noan mee **sayntoa bainay**
I'm ill.	**Mi sento male.**	mee **sayntoa marlay**
I've got a pain here.	**Ho un dolore qui.**	oa oon doa**loaray kooee**
His/Her... hurts.	**Ha male al/alla...**	ah **marlay** ahl/**ahllah**
I've got (a)...	**Ho...**	oa
headache	**il mal di testa**	eel marl dee **teh**stah
backache	**il mal di schiena**	eel marl dee **skeeainah**
fever	**la febbre**	lah **fehb**bray
sore throat	**il mal di gola**	eel marl dee **goa**lah
travel sickness	**il mal di viaggio**	eel marl dee vee**ahd**joa
I'm constipated.	**Sono costipato.**	soanoa koastee**partoa**
I've been vomiting.	**Ho vomitato.**	oa voamee**tartoa**

DOCTOR

1 — Indisposizioni

Che disturbo sente?	What's the trouble?
Dove ha male?	Where does it hurt?
Da quanto tempo ha questo dolore?	How long have you had this pain?
Da quanto tempo si sente così?	How long have you been feeling like this?
Tiri su la manica.	Roll up your sleeve
Si spogli (fino alla vita).	Please undress (to the waist)
Si tolga i pantaloni e le mutande.	Please remove your pants and shorts

DOCTOR

PATIENT

I feel…	**Mi sento…**	mee **say**ntoa
faint/dizzy	**debole/stordito**	**dai**boalay/stoar**dee**toa
nauseous	**la nausea**	lah **now**sayah
shivery	**rabbrividire**	rahbbreevee**dee**ray
I have/She has/ He has (a/an)…	**Io ho/Egli ha/ Ella ha…**	**ee**oa oa/**ay**lyee ah **ayl**lah ah
abscess	**un ascesso**	oon ah**shehss**soa
asthma	**l'asma**	**lahz**mah
boil	**un foruncolo**	oon foa**roong**koaloa
chill	**un'infreddatura**	ooneenfrayddah**too**rah
cold	**il raffreddore**	eel rahffrayd**doa**ray
constipation	**una costipazione**	**oo**nah koasteepahtsee**oa**nay
convulsions	**le convulsioni**	lay koanvoolseeoanee
cramps	**i crampi**	ee **krahm**pee
diarrhoea	**la diarrea**	lah deeah**rray**ah
fever	**la febbre**	lah **fehb**bray
haemorrhoids	**le emorroidi**	lay aymoar**roee**dee
hay fever	**la febbre del fieno**	lah **fehb**bray dayl feee**h**noa
hernia	**l'ernia**	**lehr**neeah

DOCTOR

Per favore, si sdrai qui.	Please lie down over here.
Apra la bocca.	Open your mouth
Respiri profondamente.	Breathe deeply
Tossisca, per favore.	Cough, please
Le provo la febbre.	I'll take your temperature
Le misuro la pressione del sangue.	I'm going to take your blood pressure
È la prima volta che ha questo disturbo?	Is this the first time you've had this?
Le faccio un'iniezione.	I'll give you an injection
Desidero un campione dell'urina (delle feci).	I want a specimen of your urine (stools)

PATIENT

indigestion	un'indigestione	ooneendeejaysteeoanay
inflammation of...	un'infiammazione a...	ooneenfeeahmmahtseeoanay ah
influenza	l'influenza	leenflooehntsah
morning sickness	la nausea al mattino	lah nowsayah ahl mahtteenoa
rheumatism	i reumatismi	ee rayoomahteezmee
stiff neck	il torcicollo	eel torcheekolloa
sunburn	una scottatura (di sole)	oonah skottahtoorah (dee soalay)
sunstroke	un colpo di sole	oon koalpoa dee soalay
tonsillitis	la tonsillite	lah toanseelleetay
ulcer	l'ulcera	loolchayrah
whooping cough	la pertosse	lah pairtosssay
It's nothing serious, I hope?	Non è niente di grave, spero.	noan ai neeehntay dee grarvay spayroa
I'd like you to prescribe some medicine for me.	Vorrei che mi prescrivesse delle medicine.	vorraiee kay mee prayskreevaysssay dayllay maydeecheenay

---

DOCTOR

Non è nulla di grave. — It's nothing to worry about.

Deve restare a letto per... giorni. — You must stay in bed for days.

Lei ha... — You've got...

il raffreddore/l'artrite
la polmonite/l'influenza
un avvelenamento da cibi
un'infiammazione a...
l'appendicite — a cold/arthritis
pneumonia/influenza
food poisoning
an inflammation of...
an appendicitis

Lei fuma/beve troppo. — You're smoking/drinking too much

Lei è troppo stanco. Ha bisogno di riposo. — You're over-tired You need a rest.

Voglio che vada all'ospedale per un controllo generale. — I want you to go to the hospital for a general check-up.

Le prescrivo un antibiotico. — I'll prescribe an antibiotic.

PATIENT

I'm a diabetic.	**Ho il diabete.**	oa eel deeah**beh**tay
I've a cardiac condition.	**Sono ammalato di cuore.**	**soa**noa ahmmah**lar**toa dee **kwo**ray
I had a heart attack in...	**Ho avuto un attacco cardiaco nel...**	oa ah**voo**toa oon aht**tahk**koa kahr**dee**ahkoa nayl
I'm allergic to...	**Sono allergico a...**	**soa**noa ahl**layr**jeekoa ah
This is my usual medicine.	**Questa è la mia medicina abituale.**	**koo**aystah ai lah **mee**ah maydee**chee**nah ahbee**too**arlay
I need this medicine.	**Ho bisogno di questa medicina.**	oa bee**zoa**ñoa dee **koo**aystah maydee**chee**nah
I'm expecting a baby	**Aspetto un bambino.**	ahs**payt**toa oon bahm-**bee**noa
Can I travel?	**Posso viaggiare?**	**pos**soa veeahdj**jar**ray

---

DOCTOR

Quale dose di insulina ha preso finora?	What dose of insulin are you taking?
Per iniezioni o per via orale?	Injection or oral?
Quale cura sta facendo?	What treatment have you been having?
Che medicine prende attualmente?	What medicine have you been taking?
Ha avuto un (leggero) attacco cardiaco.	You've had a (slight) heart attack.
In Italia non usiamo... Questo è molto simile.	We don't use in Italy This is very similar
Quando deve nascere il bambino?	When's the baby due?
Non può viaggiare fino al...	You can't travel until

PATIENT

Part 2 – Wounds

I've got a/an...Could you have a look at it?	**Ho...Può esaminarmi?**	oa pwo ayzahmeenarrmee
blister	**una vescica**	oonah vaysheekah
boil	**un foruncolo**	oon foaroongkoaloa
bruise	**una contusione**	oonah koantoozeeoanay
burn	**una scottatura**	oonah skottahtoorah
cut	**un taglio**	oon tarlyoa
graze	**un'escoriazione**	oonayskoareeahtseeoanay
insect bite	**una puntura d'insetto**	oonah poontoorah deensehttoa
lump	**un bernoccolo**	oon bayrnokkoaloa
rash	**un esantema**	oon ayzahntehmah
sting	**una puntura**	oonah poontoorah
swelling	**una tumefazione**	oonah toomayfahtseeoanay
wound	**una ferita**	oonah fayreetah
I can't move my... It hurts.	**Non posso muovere... Mi fa male.**	noan posssoa mwovayray...mee fah marlay

---

DOCTOR

2 – Ferite

(Non) è infetto.	It's (not) infected.
Ha uno spostamento vertebrale.	You've got a slipped disc.
Voglio che faccia una radiografia.	I want you to have an X-ray.
È...	It's...
rotto/slogato	broken/sprained
Ha...	It's...
una lussazione/una lacerazione	dislocated/torn
Ha uno strappo muscolare.	You've pulled a muscle.
Le darò un antisettico.	I'll give you an antiseptic.
Ritorni fra...giorni.	I want you to come and see me in...day's time.

DOCTOR

PATIENT

Part 3 – Nervous tension

I'm in a nervous state.	**Sono molto nervoso.**	soanoa moaltoa nehrvoassoa
I'm feeling depressed.	**Mi sento depresso.**	mee sayntoa dayprehsssoa
I want some sleeping pills.	**Vorrei dei sonniferi.**	vorraiee daiee soannee-fayree
I can't eat.	**Non ho appetito.**	noan oa ahppayteetoa
I can't sleep.	**Non riesco a dormire.**	noan reeehskoa ah doarmeeray
I'm having nightmares	**Soffro di incubi.**	soaffroa dee eengkoobee
Can you prescribe a...?	**Può prescrivermi...?**	pwo prayskreevayrmee
sedative tranquilizer	**un sedativo** **un tranquillante**	oon saydahteevoa oon trahngkooeellahntay

---

DOCTOR

3 – Stati ansiosi

Soffre di tensione nervosa.	You're suffering from nervous tension.
Ha bisogno di riposo.	You need a rest.
Quali compresse ha preso?	What pills have you been taking?
Quante al giorno?	How many a day?
Da quanto tempo si sente così?	How long have you been feeling like this?
Le prescrivo delle compresse.	I'll prescribe some pills.
Le prescrivo un sedativo.	I'll give you a sedative.

PATIENT

Prescriptions and dosage

What kind of medicine is this?	**Che genere di medicina è?**	kay **jeh**nayray dee maydee**chee**nah ai
How many times a day should I take it?	**Quante volte al giorno devo prenderla?**	**kwahn**tay **vol**tay ahl **joar**noa **day**voa **prehn**dayrlah
Must I swallow them whole?	**Devo inghiottirle intere?**	**day**voa eenggeeoat**teer**lay **een**tayray

Fee

How much do I owe you?	**Quanto le devo?**	**kwahn**toa lay **day**voa
Do I pay you now or will you send me your bill?	**Pago subito o mi manda la nota?**	**par**goa **soo**beetoa oa mee **mahn**dah lah **no**tah
Thanks for your help, Doctor.	**Grazie mille, dottore.**	**grah**tseeay **meel**lay doat**toa**ray

DOCTOR

Ricette e dosi

Prenda...cucchiaini da tè di questa medicina ogni...ore.	Take...teaspoons of this medicine every...hours.
Prenda...compresse con un bicchiere d'acqua...	Take...pills with a glass of water...
...volte al giorno	...times a day
prima dei pasti	before each meal
dopo i pasti	after each meal
fra un pasto e l'altro	between meals
al mattino	in the morning
alla sera	at night

L'onorario

Sono..., per favore.	That's..., please.
Paghi ora, per favore.	Please pay me now.
Le manderò il conto.	I'll send you a bill.

FOR NUMBERS, see page 175

DOCTOR

Dentist

Can you recommend a good dentist?	**Può consigliarmi un buon dentista?**	pwo koanseelyaarmee oon bwawn daynteestah
Can I make an (urgent) appointment to see Dr....?	**Desidero un appuntamento (urgente) con il dottor...**	dayzeedayroa oon ahppoontahmayntoa (oorjehntay) kon eel doattoar
Can't you possibly make it earlier than that?	**Non è possibile prima?**	noan ai poasssseebeelay preemah
I've a toothache.	**Ho mal di denti.**	oa marl dee dehntee
I've an abscess.	**Ho un ascesso.**	oa oon ahshehsssoa
This tooth hurts.	**Mi fa male questo dente.**	mee fah marlay kooaystoa dehntay
at the top	**in alto**	een ahltoa
at the bottom	**in basso**	een bahsssoa
in the front	**davanti**	dahvahntee
at the back	**dietro**	deeehtroa
Can you fix it temporarily?	**Può curarlo provvisoriamente?**	pwo koorarrloa proavveezoareeahmayntay
I don't want it extracted.	**Non voglio un'estrazione.**	noan volyoa oonaystrahtseeoanay
I've lost a filling.	**L'otturazione si è staccata.**	loattoorahtseeoanay see ai stahkkartah
The gum...	**La gengiva...**	lah jaynjeevah
is very sore	**è molto infiammata**	ai moaltoa eenfeeahmmartah
is bleeding	**sanguina**	sahnggooeeenah

Dentures

I've broken this denture.	**Ho rotto questa dentiera.**	oa roattoa kooaystah daynteeehrah
Can you repair this denture?	**Può ripararmi questa dentiera?**	pwo reepahrarrmee kooaystah daynteeehrah
When will it be ready?	**Quando sarà pronta?**	kwahndoa sahrah proantah

Optician

I've broken my glasses.	**Ho rotto gli occhiali.**	oa roattoa lyee okkeearlee
Can you repair them for me?	**Può ripararmeli?**	pwo reepahrarrmaylee
When will they be ready?	**Quando saranno pronti?**	kwahndoa sahrahnnoa proantee
Can you change the lenses?	**Può cambiare le lenti?**	pwo kahmbeearray lay lehntee
I want tinted lenses.	**Desidero delle lenti colorate.**	dayzeedayroa dayllay lehntee koaloarartay
I want contact lenses.	**Desidero delle lenti a contatto.**	dayzeedayroa dayllay lehntee ah koantahttoa
I'd like to buy a pair of binoculars.	**Vorrei acquistare un binocolo.**	vorraiee akkooeestarray oon beenokoaloa
I'd like to buy a pair of sun-glasses.	**Vorrei degli occhiali da sole.**	vorraiee daylyee okkeearlee dah soalay
How much do I owe you?	**Quanto le devo?**	kwahntoa lay dayvoa
Do I pay you now or will you send me your bill?	**Pago subito o mi manda la fattura?**	pargoa soobeetoa oa mee mahndah lah fahttoorah

OPTICIAN

FOR NUMBERS, see page 175

Reference section

Where do you come from?

This page will help you to explain where you're from, where you've been, and where you're going.

Africa	**Africa**	arfreekah
Algeria	**Algeria**	ahljayreeah
Asia	**Asia**	arzeeah
Australia	**Australia**	owstrarlyah
Austria	**Austria**	owstreeah
Belgium	**Belgio**	behljoa
Canada	**Canadà**	kahnahdah
China	**Cina**	cheenah
England	**Inghilterra**	eenggeeltehrrah
Europe	**Europa**	ayooropah
France	**Francia**	frahnchah
Germany	**Germania**	jayrmarneeah
Great Britain	**Gran Bretagna**	grahn braytarñah
Greece	**Grecia**	graichah
Holland	**Olanda**	olahndah
Ireland	**Irlanda**	eerlahndah
Italy	**Italia**	eetarlyah
Japan	**Giappone**	jahpponay
Malta	**Malta**	mahltah
Morocco	**Marocco**	mahrokkoa
New Zealand	**Nuova Zelanda**	nwawvah tsaylahndah
North America	**America del Nord**	ahmaireekah dayl nord
San Marino	**San Marino**	sahn mahreenoa
Scandinavia	**Scandinavia**	skahndeenarveeah
Scotland	**Scozia**	skotseeah
Sicily	**Sicilia**	seecheelyah
South Africa	**Africa del Sud**	arfreekah dayl sood
South America	**America del Sud**	ahmaireekah dayl sood
Soviet Union	**Unione Sovietica**	ooneeoanay soaveeehteekah
Spain	**Spagna**	sparñah
Switzerland	**Svizzera**	sveettsayrah
Tunisia	**Tunisia**	tooneezeeah
United States	**Stati Uniti**	startee ooneetee
Vatican City	**Città del Vaticano**	cheettah dayl vahteekarnoa
Wales	**Galles**	gahllayss
Yugoslavia	**Jugoslavia**	eeoogoaslarveeah

Numbers

0	**zero**	**dzeh**roa
1	**uno**	oonoa
2	**due**	**doo**ay
3	**tre**	tray
4	**quattro**	**kwaht**troa
5	**cinque**	**cheeng**kooay
6	**sei**	**seh**ee
7	**sette**	**seht**tay
8	**otto**	**ott**oa
9	**nove**	**naw**vay
10	**dieci**	**deeai**chee
11	**undici**	**oon**deechee
12	**dodici**	**doa**deechee
13	**tredici**	**tray**deechee
14	**quattordici**	kwaht**tor**deechee
15	**quindici**	koo**een**deechee
16	**sedici**	**say**deechee
17	**diciassette**	deechahss**seht**tay
18	**diciotto**	deech**ott**ao
19	**diciannove**	deechahn**naw**vay
20	**venti**	**vayn**tee
21	**ventuno**	vayn**too**noa
22	**ventidue**	vayntee**doo**ay
23	**ventitre**	vayntee**tray**
24	**ventiquattro**	vayntee**kwaht**troa
25	**venticinque**	vayntee**cheeng**kooay
26	**ventisei**	vayntee**seh**ee
27	**ventisette**	vayntee**seht**tay
28	**ventotto**	vayn**tott**oa
29	**ventinove**	vayntee**naw**vay
30	**trenta**	**trayn**tah
31	**trentuno**	traynt**oo**noa
32	**trentadue**	trayntah**doo**ay
33	**trentatre**	trayntat**ray**
40	**quaranta**	kwah**rahn**tah
41	**quarantuno**	kwahrahn**too**noa
42	**quarantadue**	kwahrahntah**doo**ay
43	**quarantatre**	kwahrahntah**tray**
50	**cinquanta**	cheeng**kwahn**tah
51	**cinquantuno**	cheengkwahn**too**noa
52	**cinquantadue**	cheengkwahntah**doo**ay
53	**cinquantatre**	cheengkwahntah**tray**
60	**sessanta**	saysss**sahn**tah
61	**sessantuno**	saysssahn**too**noa

62	**sessantadue**	saysssahntahdooay
63	**sessantatre**	saysssahntahtray
70	**settanta**	sayttahntah
71	**settantuno**	sayttahntoonoa
72	**settantadue**	sayttahntahdooay
73	**settantatre**	sayttahntahtray
80	**ottanta**	oattahntah
81	**ottantuno**	ottahntoonoa
82	**ottantadue**	ottahntahdooay
83	**ottantatre**	ottahntahtray
90	**novanta**	noavahntah
91	**novantuno**	noavahntoonoa
92	**novantadue**	noavahntahdooay
93	**novantatre**	noavahntahtray
100	**cento**	chehntoa
101	**centouno**	chehntoaoonoa
102	**centodue**	chehntoadooay
110	**centodieci**	chehntoadeeaichee
120	**centoventi**	chehntoavayntee
130	**centotrenta**	chehntoatrayntah
140	**centoquaranta**	chehntoakwahrahntah
150	**centocinquanta**	chehntoacheengkwahntah
160	**centosessanta**	chehntoassaysssahntah
170	**centosettanta**	chehntoassayttahntah
180	**centottanta**	chehntottahntah
190	**centonovanta**	chehntoanoavahntah
200	**duecento**	dooaychehntoa
300	**trecento**	traychehntoa
400	**quattrocento**	kwahttroachehntoa
500	**cinquecento**	cheengkwaychehntoa
600	**seicento**	sayeechehntoa
700	**settecento**	sehttaychehntoa
800	**ottocento**	ottochehntoa
900	**novecento**	noavaychehntoa
1000	**mille**	meellay
1100	**millecento**	meellaychehntoa
1200	**milleduecento**	meellaydooaychehntoa
2000	**duemila**	dooaymeelah
5000	**cinquemila**	cheengkooaymeelah
10,000	**diecimila**	deeaicheemeelah
50,000	**cinquantamila**	cheengkwahntahmeelah
100,000	**centomila**	chehntoameelah
1,000,000	**un milione**	oon meelyoanay
1,000,000,000	**un miliardo**	oon meelyarrdoa

first	primo	preemoa
second	secondo	saykoandoa
third	terzo	tehrtsoa
fourth	quarto	kwarrtoa
fifth	quinto	kooeentoa
sixth	sesto	sehstoa
seventh	settimo	sehtteemoa
eighth	ottavo	ottarvoa
ninth	nono	nonoa
tenth	decimo	dehcheemoa
once	una volta	oonah voltah
twice	due volte	dooay voltay
three times	tre volte	tray voltay
a half	un mezzo	oon mehddzoa
half a...	mezzo...	mehddzoa
half of...	metà di...	maytah dee
half (adj)	mezzo	mehddzoa
a quarter	un quarto	oon kwarrtoa
one third	un terzo	oon tehrtsoa
a pair of	un paio di	oon pareeoa dee
a dozen	una dozzina	oonah doaddzeenah

1977 **millenovecentosettantasette**
(meellay-noavaychehntoa-sayttahtahsehttay)

1978 **millenovecentosettantaotto**
(meellay-noavaychehntoa-sayttahtahottoa)

1979 **millenovecentosettantanove**
(meellay-noavaychehntoa-sayttahtahnawvay)

1980 **millenovecentottanta**
(meellay-noavaychehnt-ottahntah)

Time

**le dodici
e un quarto**
(lay **doa**deechee ay oon
kwahrtoa)

l'una e venti
(**l**oonah ay **vayn**tee)

**le due
e venticinque**
(lay **doo**ay ay
vaynteec**heeng**kooay)

le tre e mezzo
(lay tray ay **mehd**dzoa)

**le quattro
e trentacinque**
(lay **kwaht**troa
ay trayntah**cheeng**kooay)

**le cinque
e quaranta**
(lay **cheeng**kooay
ay kwah**rahn**tah)

**le sette
meno un quarto**
(lay **seht**tay **mai**noa oon
kwahrtoa)

le otto meno dieci
(lay **ot**toa **mai**noa
deeaichee)

**le nove
meno cinque**
(lay **naw**vay **mai**noa
cheengkooay)

le dieci
(lay **dee**aichee)

le undici e cinque
(lay **oon**deechee ay
cheengkooay)

le dodici e dieci
(lay **doa**deechee ay
deeaichee)

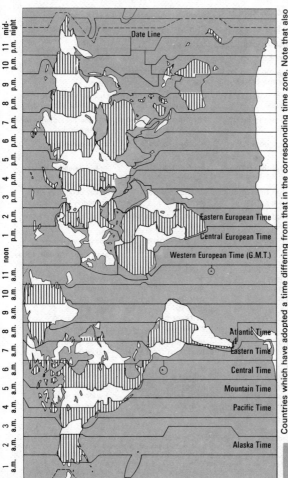

REFERENCE SECTION

Date Line

11 mid- night

10 p.m.

9 p.m.

8 p.m.

7 p.m.

6 p.m.

5 p.m.

4 p.m.

3 p.m.

2 p.m.

1 p.m.

noon

11 a.m.

10 a.m.

9 a.m.

8 a.m.

7 a.m.

6 a.m.

5 a.m.

4 a.m.

3 a.m.

2 a.m.

1 a.m.

Eastern European Time

Central European Time

Western European Time (G.M.T.)

Atlantic Time

Eastern Time

Central Time

Mountain Time

Pacific Time

Alaska Time

Countries which have adopted a time differing from that in the corresponding time zone. Note that also in the USSR, official time is one hour ahead of the time in each corresponding time zone. In summer, numerous countries advance time one hour ahead of standard time.

What time is it?

What time is it?	**Che ore sono?**	kay oaray soanao
It's one o'clock.	**È l'una.**	ai loonah
It's three o'clock.	**Sono le tre.**	soanoa lay tray
Excuse me. Can you tell me the time?	**Scusi, può dirmi l'ora?**	skoozee pwo deermee loarah
I'll meet you at... tomorrow.	**Ci incontreremo domani alle...**	chee eengkontrayraymoa doamarnee ahllay
I'm sorry I'm late.	**Mi dispiace, sono in ritardo.**	mee deespeearchay soanoa een reetahrdoa
At what time does... open?	**A che ora apre...?**	ah kay oarah arpray
At what time does... close?	**A che ora chiude...?**	ah kay oarah keeooday
At what time should I be there?	**A che ora devo venire?**	ah kay oarah dayvoa vayneeray
At what time will you be there?	**A che ora verrete?**	ah kay oarah vayrraytay
Can I come...?	**Posso venire...?**	posssoa vayneeray
at 8 o'clock/at 2:30	**alle 8/alle 2 e mezzo***	ahllay ottoa/ahllay dooay ay mehddzoa
after (prep.)	**dopo**	dawpoa
afterwards	**dopo**	dawpoa
before	**prima**	preemah
early	**presto**	prehstoa
in time	**in tempo**	een tehmpoa
late	**tardi**	tahrdee
midnight	**mezzanotte**	mehddzahnottay
noon	**mezzogiorno**	mehddzoajoarnoa
hour	**ora**	oarah
minute	**minuto**	meenootoa
second	**secondo**	saykoandoa
quarter of an hour	**quarto d'ora**	kwahrtoa doarah
half an hour	**mezz'ora**	mehddzoarah

* In ordinary conversation, time is expressed as shown here (see also page 178). However, official time uses a 24-hour clock which means that after noon hours are counted from 13 to 24. For instance, 13.15 would be 1.15 p.m. for us and 20h.30 is 8.30 p.m. At midnight time returns to 0 so that 12.17 a.m. is written 0h.27.

Days

What day is it today?	**Che giorno è oggi?**	kay joarnao ai odjee
Sunday	**domenica**	doamayneekah
Monday	**lunedì**	loonaydee
Tuesday	**martedì**	mahrtaydee
Wednesday	**mercoledì**	mehrkoalaydee
Thursday	**giovedì**	joavaydee
Friday	**venerdì**	vaynayrdee
Saturday	**sabato**	sarbahtoa

Note: The names of days and months are not capitalized in Italian.

in the morning	**al mattino**	ahl mahtteenoa
during the day	**durante il giorno**	doorahntay eel joarnoa
in the afternoon	**nel pomeriggio**	nayl poamayreedjoa
in the evening	**alla sera**	ahllah sayrah
at night	**la notte**	lah nottay
yesterday	**ieri**	eeairee
today	**oggi**	odjee
tomorrow	**domani**	doamarnee
the day before	**il giorno prima**	eel joarnoa preemah
the next day	**il giorno seguente**	eel joarnoa saygooayntay
two days ago	**due giorni fa**	dooay joarnee fah
in three days' time	**in tre giorni**	een tray joarnee
last week	**la settimana scorsa**	lah saytteemarnah skoarsah
next week	**la settimana prossima**	lah saytteemarnah prossseemah
for a fortnight (two weeks)	**per due settimane**	pair dooay saytteemarnay
birthday	**il compleanno**	eel koamplayahnnoa
day	**il giorno**	eel joarnoa
day off	**il giorno di riposo**	eel joarnoa dee reepossoa
holiday	**il giorno festivo**	eel joarnoa faysteevoa
holidays	**le vacanze**	lay vahkahntsay
month	**il mese**	eel maissay
school holidays	**le vacanze scolastiche**	lay vahkahntsay skolarsteekay
vacation	**le vacanze**	lay vahkahntsay
week	**la settimana**	lah saytteemarnah
weekday	**il giorno della settimana**	eel joarnoa dayllah saytteemarnah
weekend	**il fine settimana**	eel feenay saytteemarnah
working day	**il giorno feriale**	eel joarnoa fayreearlay

Months

January	**gennaio**	jai**nnig**hoa
February	**febbraio**	fehb**brig**hoa
March	**marzo**	**mahrt**soa
April	**aprile**	ah**pree**lay
May	**maggio**	**mahd**joa
June	**giugno**	**joo**ñoa
July	**luglio**	**lool**yoa
August	**agosto**	ah**goas**toa
September	**settembre**	say**ttehm**bray
October	**ottobre**	oat**toa**bray
November	**novembre**	noa**vehm**bray
December	**dicembre**	dee**chem**bray

since June	**da giugno**	dah **joo**ñoa
during the month of August	**durante il mese di agosto**	doo**rahn**tay eel **mais**say dee ah**goas**toa
last month	**il mese scorso**	eel **mais**say **skoar**soa
next month	**il mese prossimo**	eel **mais**say **pross**seemoa
the month before	**il mese prima**	eel **mais**say **pree**mah
the next month	**il mese dopo**	eel **mais**say **daw**poa

July 1	**il primo luglio**	eel **pree**moa **lool**yoa
March 17	**il diciassette marzo**	eel deechahss**seht**tay **mahrt**soa

Letter headings are written thus:

Rome, August 17, 1977	**Roma, 17 agosto 1977**
Milan, July 1, 1977	**Milano, 1 luglio 1977**

Seasons

spring	**la primavera**	lah preemah**vay**rah
summer	**l'estate**	lays**tar**tay
autumn	**l'autunno**	low**toon**noa
winter	**l'inverno**	leen**vehr**noa

in spring	**in primavera**	een preemah**vay**rah
during the summer	**durante l'estate**	doo**rahn**tay lays**tar**tay
in autumn	**in autunno**	een ow**toon**noa
during the winter	**durante l'inverno**	doo**rahn**tay leen**vehr**noa

Public holidays

Holidays vary from one region to the other. But only those days are noted below that are national holidays, when all schools, banks, stores, factories and offices are closed. (I = Italy, CH = Switzerland.)

January 1	**Primo dell'Anno**	New Year's Day	I CH
January 2			CH*
January 6	**Epifania di N.S.**	Epiphany	I
April 25	**Anniversario della Liberazione (1945)**	Liberation Day	I
May 1	**Festa del Lavoro**	Labour Day	I
June 2	**Proclamazione della Repubblica**	Inauguration of the Republic	I
June 29	**S.S. Pietro e Paolo**	Saints Peter and Paul	I
August 15	**Assunzione di M.V.**	Assumption Day	I
November 1	**Tutti i Santi**	All Saints'Day	I
November 4	**Anniversario della Vittoria (1918)**	Victory Day	I
December 8	**Immacolata Concezione**	Immaculate Conception	I
December 25	**Natale**	Christmas Day	I CH
December 26	**S. Stefano**	St. Stephen	I CH*
Movable dates:	**Lunedì dell'Angelo**	Easter Monday	I CH
	Ascensione di N.S.	Ascension Thursday	I CH
	Corpus Domini	Corpus Christi	I
	Venerdì Santo	Good Friday	CH*
	Lunedì di Pentecoste	Whit Monday	CH

* Most cantons

Seasonal temperatures

	Milan	Rome	Palermo
January	39°F	52°F	57°F
April	66	66	68
July	86	88	88
October	63	70	75

Abbreviations

a.	**arrivo**	arrival
a.C.	**avanti Cristo**	B.C.
A.C.I.	**Automobile Club d'Italia**	Automobile Association of Italy
A.C.S.	**Automobile Club Svizzero**	Automobile Association of Switzerland
a.D.	**anno Domini**	A.D.
A.G.I.P	**Azienda Generale Italiana Petroli**	Italian Petroleum Company
alt.	**altitudine**	altitude
ca	**circa**	approximately
C.I.T.	**Compagnia Italiana Turismo**	Italian Travel Agency
C.P.	**casella postale**	post office box
C.so	**corso**	avenue
d.C.	**dopo Cristo**	A.D.
ecc.	**eccetera**	etc.
EE	**Escursionisti Esteri**	number car plates for foreigners
E.N.I.T.	**Ente Nazionale Industrie Turistiche**	National Tourist Organization
F.F.S.	**Ferrovie Federali Svizzere**	Swiss Federal Railways
F.S.	**Ferrovie dello Stato**	National Railways
I.V.A.	**Imposta sul Valore Aggiunto**	value added tax (sales tax)
Mil.	**militare**	military
p.	**partenza**	departure
P.T.	**Poste & Telecomunicazioni**	Post & Telecommunications
P.za	**piazza**	square
R.A.I.	**Radio Audizioni Italiane**	Italian Broadcasting Company
Rep.	**Repubblica**	republic
sec.	**secolo**	century
Sig.	**Signor**	Mr.
Sig.na	**Signorina**	Miss
Sig.ra	**Signora**	Mrs.
s.p.a.	**società per azioni**	Ltd, Inc
S.P.Q.R.	**Senatus Populusque Romanus**	The Senate and the People of Rome (Latin)
T.C.I.	**Touring Club Italiano**	Italian Touring Association
T.C.S.	**Touring Club Svizzero**	Swiss Touring Association
V.le	**viale**	avenue
V.U.	**Vigili Urbani**	city police

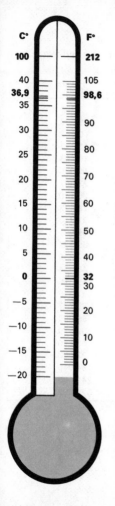

Conversion tables

Centimetres and inches

To change centimetres into inches, multiply by .39.

To change inches into centimetres, multiply by 2.54.

	in.	feet	yards
1 mm	0,039	0,003	0,001
1 cm	0,39	0,03	0,01
1 dm	3,94	0,32	0,10
1 m	39,40	3,28	1,09

	mm	cm	m
1 in.	25,4	2,54	0,025
1 ft.	304,8	30,48	0,304
1 yd.	914,4	91,44	0,914

(32 metres = 35 yards)

Temperature

To convert Centigrade into degrees Fahrenheit, multiply Centigrade by 1.8 and add 32.

To convert degrees Fahrenheit into Centigrade, subtract 32 from Fahrenheit and divide by 1.8.

Metres and feet

The figure in the middle stands for both metres and feet, e.g.,
1 metre = 3.28 feet and 1 foot = 0.30 m.

Metres		Feet
0.30	1	3.281
0.61	2	6.563
0.91	3	9.843
1.22	4	13.124
1.52	5	16.403
1.83	6	19.686
2.13	7	22.967
2.44	8	26.248
2.74	9	29.529
3.05	10	32.810
3.35	11	36.091
3.66	12	39.372
3.96	13	42.635
4.27	14	45.934
4.57	15	49.215
4.88	16	52.496
5.18	17	55.777
5.49	18	59.058
5.79	19	62.339
6.10	20	65.620
7.62	25	82.023
15.24	50	164.046
22.86	75	246.069
30.48	100	328.092

Other conversion charts

Weight conversion

The figure in the middle stands for both kilograms and pounds, e.g., 1 kilogram = 2.20 pounds and 1 pound = 0.45 kilograms.

Kilograms (kg.)		Avoirdupois pounds
0.45	1	2.205
0.90	2	4.405
1.35	3	6.614
1.80	4	8.818
2.25	5	11.023
2.70	6	13.227
3.15	7	15.432
3.60	8	17.636
4.05	9	19.840
4.50	10	22.045
6.75	15	33.068
9.00	20	44.889
11.25	25	55.113
22.50	50	110.225
33.75	75	165.338
45.00	100	220.450

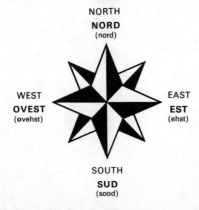

NORTH
NORD
(nord)

WEST
OVEST
(ovehst)

EAST
EST
(ehst)

SOUTH
SUD
(sood)

REFERENCE SECTION

What does that sign mean ?

You're sure to encounter some of these signs or notices on your trip.

Ascensore	Lift (elevator)
Attenti al cane	Beware of the dog
Caldo	Hot
Cassiere	Cashier's
Chiudo	Closed
Da affittare	To let, for hire
Entrare senza bussare	Enter without knocking
Entrata	Entrance
Entrata libera	Free entrance
Freddo	Cold
I trasgressori saranno puniti a norma di legge	Trespassers will be prosecuted
Informazioni	Information
In vendita	For sale
Libero	Vacant
Occupato	Occupied
Pericolo	Danger
Pericolo di morte	Danger of death
Pista per ciclisti	Path for cyclists
Privato	Private
Prudenza	Caution
Riservato	Reserved
Saldi	Sales
Signore	Ladies
Signori	Gentlemen
Spingere	Push
Strada privata	Private road
Suonare, per favore	Please ring
Svendita	Sales
Tirare	Pull
Uscita	Exit
Uscita di emergenza	Emergency exit
Vietato...	...forbidden
Vietato fumare	No smoking
Vietato l'ingresso	No entrance
Vietato toccare	Do not touch

Emergency

By the time the emergency is upon you it's too late to turn to this page to find the Italian for "I'll scream if you...". So have a look at this short list beforehand—and, if you want to be on the safe side, learn the expressions shown in capitals.

Be quick	**Faccia presto**	**faht**chah **preh**stoa
Call the police	**Chiami la polizia**	kee**ar**mee la poalee**tsee**ah
CAREFUL	**ATTENTO**	ah**tteh**ntoa
Come here	**Venga qui**	**vay**nggah kooee
Come in	**Entri**	**ay**ntree
Danger	**Pericolo**	payree**koa**loa
Fire	**Fuoco**	**fwaw**koa
Gas	**Gas**	gaz
Get a doctor	**Chiami un medico**	kee**ar**mee oon **mai**deekoa
Go away	**Se ne vada**	say nay **var**dah
HELP	**AIUTO**	i**ghoo**toa
Get help quickly	**Chiami dei soccorsi, presto**	kee**ar**mee **dai**ee soa**kkoar**see **preh**stoa
I'm ill	**Mi sento male**	mee **sayn**toa **mar**lay
I'm lost	**Mi sono perso**	mee **soa**noa **pehr**soa
I've lost my	**Ho perso...**	oa **pehr**soa
Keep your hands to yourself	**Tenga le mani a posto**	**tayng**gah lay **mar**nee ah **poa**stoa
Leave me alone	**Mi lasci in pace**	mee **lar**shee een **par**chay
Lie down	**Si metta a terra**	see **mayt**tah ah **tayr**rah
Listen	**Ascolti**	as**koal**tee
Listen to me	**Mi ascolti**	mee as**koal**tee
LOOK	**GUARDI**	**gwahr**dee
Look out	**Stia attento**	**stee**ah ah**tteh**ntoa
POLICE	**POLIZIA**	poalee**tsee**ah
Quick	**Presto**	**preh**stoa
STOP	**STOP**	stop
Stop here	**Si fermi là**	see **fayr**mee lah
Stop that man	**Fermate quell'uomo**	fayr**mar**tay kooayll**wo**moa
Stop thief	**Fermate il ladro**	fayr**mar**tay eel **lar**droa
Stop or I'll scream	**Si fermi o grido**	see **fayr**mee o **gree**doa

FOR CAR ACCIDENTS, see page 150

REFERENCE SECTION

Index

Quick reference page

Please	**Per favore.**	pair fahvoaray
Thank you	**Grazie.**	grahtseeay
Yes/No	**Sì/No.**	see/no
Excuse me	**Mi scusi.**	mee skoozee
Waiter, please	**Cameriere, per favore.**	kahmayreeehray pair fahvoaray
How much is that?	**Quant'è?**	kwahntai
Where are the toilets?	**Dove sono i gabinetti?**	doavay soanoa ee gahbeenayttee

Toilets

SIGNORI/UOMINI
(seeñoaree/womeenee)

SIGNORE/DONNE
(seeñoaray/donnay)

Could you tell me?	**Può dirmi...?**	pwo deermee
where/when/why	**dove/quando/perchè**	doavay/kwahndoa/pehrkay
Help me, please	**Per favore, mi aiuti.**	pair fahvoaray mee ighootee
Where is the... consulate?	**Dov'è il consolato...?**	doavai eel koansoalartoa
American	**americano**	ahmayreekarnoa
British	**inglese**	eengglayssay
Canadian	**canadese**	kahnahdayssay
What does this mean? I don't understand	**Cosa significa questo? Non capisco.**	kawsah seeñeefeekah kooaystoa? noan kahpeeskoa
Do you speak English?	**Parla inglese?**	pahrlah eengglayssay

REFERENCE SECTION